A Daily Devotional for Drawing Closer to the Heart of God

Centering Prayers *for* Women

PETER TRABEN HAAS
FOREWORD BY JUDITH VALENTE

PARACLETE PRESS
BREWSTER, MASSACHUSETTS

2023 First Printing

Centering Prayers for Women: A Daily Devotional for Drawing Closer to the Heart of God

ISBN 978-1-64060-858-0

Library of Congress Cataloging-in-Publication Data
Names: Haas, Peter Traben, author.
Title: Centering prayers for women : a daily devotional for drawing closer to the heart of God / Peter Traben Haas.
Description: Brewster, Massachusetts : Paraclete Press, 2023. | Summary: "365 daily words especially written for women. These devotions will take you deeper into the heart of God's love, deeper into the Spirit's care, and deeper into silence"-- Provided by publisher.
Identifiers: LCCN 2022042306 (print) | LCCN 2022042307 (ebook) | ISBN 9781640608580 | ISBN 9781640608597 (epub) | ISBN 9781640608603 (pdf)
Subjects: LCSH: Christian women--Prayers and devotions.
Classification: LCC BV4844 .H23 2023 (print) | LCC BV4844 (ebook) | DDC 242/.643--dc23/eng/20221129
LC record available at https://lccn.loc.gov/2022042306
LC ebook record available at https://lccn.loc.gov/2022042307

10 9 8 7 6 5 4 3 2 1

Published by Paraclete Press
Brewster, Massachusetts
www.paracletepress.com

Printed in India

To Marcia,
queen of my heart.

And Mother Mary,
first to feel Christ's heartbeat within.

Source

Our Source of Life:

We come from you and return to you,
and in between
we learn how to love you, love others, and love ourselves.

You are with us, and
beyond the gray veil of perception,
we are with you.

Sustainer

Measured against the sky, our lives light up with meaning.

A vast moment hovering on a fire-line horizon.

Opening to the unknown,
the future,
the endless prairie of Being and Becoming.

I wake from the dream of forgetfulness,
see your face,
and remember who I am.

CONTENTS

FOREWORD

Someone who has had a profound effect on my spiritual journey is Brother Paul Quenon, a member of the Cistercian Order of the Strict Observance, also known as the Trappists. The work of Trappist monks isn't an active apostolic mission. It is to pray. Community prayer begins with Vigils at 3:15 in the morning. The monks stop for prayer seven more times during the day. The hours between Vigils and Lauds at 5:45 a.m. are given over to meditation and sacred reading. The monks observe long periods of silence each day.

Brother Paul entered the Trappists at age 17 and has been a member of the monastic community of the Abbey of Gethsemani outside of Louisville for 65 years. You would expect him to be a prayer "master." Instead, Brother Paul often says he is not sure he now knows more about prayer and meditation than when he entered the Trappists. This is a startling admission, but an authentic one from someone who seeks to live by the Truth. Perhaps better than most of us, he understands the true nature of prayer.

We often hear of prayer referred to as a "practice," as if it is something we can master by repeated effort, the way one learns to play the violin or speak a foreign language. Prayer, though, is something far more mysterious. As Brother Paul, and all the great mystics will tell us, prayer is more than a practice. It is an experience. It is what Brother Paul calls "staying present to the Presence." As such, prayer is never static. It changes for us day to day as the will of God moves us. Once when Brother Paul was frustrated about his lack of concentration at prayer and daily meditation, he asked his spiritual director what might be going on. "Maybe that is the way the Lord wants it," the director responded. Maybe Christ comes in just such poverty of spirit. Or as Thomas Merton, Brother Paul's first spiritual director once said, "Christ always seeks the straw of the most desolate cribs to make his Bethlehem."

Those of us who engage in Centering Prayer know that it isn't about words or feelings. It is about being "present to the Presence." Still, it helps to have a set of written words that can draw us into the experience of prayer. This is the gift that Peter Traben Haas offers us. The words come from deep within the heart of one who has spent considerable time in the company of the Presence. As Peter says in his own words, "May each page be a kind of face to you where you can turn to speak and be spoken to—words to take you deeper into the heart of God's love, and words to take you deeper into the presence of Spirit's care, and words to take you deeper into the silence."

The prayers in this volume are written like poems, drawing us to look more deeply into ourselves and the world around us. They call us to what St. Bernard of Clairvaux referred to as "the real behind the real." We can use these words as Lectio Divina, by choosing to focus on a sentence, a phrase or a word, turning it over in our mind, making of it our own prayer and then resting silently with it in contemplation so it might seep into the heart. We can take a word from one of these prayers and make it our word for centering prayer. We can start and end our day with these prayers, like a pair of bookends. We can write each day's prayer down on a sheet of paper and pull it out periodically throughout our day as a means to a sacred pause.

I love that the book is organized by month. So many times, the seasons race by us without our seeming to notice them. By the time we do, the experience is lost. "It was May before my / attention turned / to spring and / my word I said / to the southern slopes / I've / missed it" the poet A. R. Ammons writes in a lovely little poem called "Eyesight." Simone Weil once described prayer as an intense form of paying attention. These prayer-poems help to ensure we remain awake and attentive.

A word about the title of the book, which announces it as centering prayers for women. True, women attend spiritual retreats in far greater numbers than men and are likely the majority in most Scripture studies and centering prayer or Lectio Divina groups. Still, this book is for everyone. It is for those already familiar with "deep silent prayer," as Haas describes it, and those still seeking to make prayer a regular part of their lives as "a breath of a quiet" in the whirl of our busy days.

Many books purport to be prayer "aids," but I have found few that are as moving, as beautifully written, or as penetrating to the deep heart's core. I hope this new edition of Centering Prayers will become for you a soul friend, allowing you to awaken to who you truly are. For as Merton, my friend Brother Paul's original spiritual director once wrote, prayer is not only the lifting up of the mind and heart to God, "it is also the response to God within us, the discovery of God within us; it leads ultimately to the discovery and fulfillment of our own true being in God." May it be so for you.

—Judith Valente, journalist, poet, and author of many titles, including *How to Live* and *How to Be*

PREFACE TO THE FIRST EDITION

Be a student of that vibrant edge where our inner life meets the world . . . where we all live on [the] shore between the depths of being and the dangers of experience.
—Mark Nepo, *The Exquisite Risk*

I feel particularly grateful to be writing this preface from the St. Albertino guest room at the New Camaldoli Hermitage in Big Sur, California. I write with a majestic view of the Pacific Ocean—today, an opaque blue capped with white runners as far as I can see from this high hillside vantage. Silence surrounds me, except for the faint and constant roar of the ocean that sounds to me like a distant highway. Of course, it's not the sound of cars and traffic to which I am so accustomed, living in the city. Rather, it is the sound of the sea singing its praises as it meets the end of its world and the beginning of ours.

I have come to the Benedictine hermitage as an interlude. I recently left a beloved pastoral role in Austin, Texas, to begin a new pastorate in Waterloo, Iowa. Like the liminal meeting place of sea and land, I too am in between the boundaries of ending and beginning. And so, I have retreated to the silence in a place of vast beauty.

Here in the silence grace has ministered to me. Both tears and laughter have bubbled up in my prayer times as I recall the life I am leaving behind. I peer across the sea and find myself pondering all that was and also what might be.

From the solitude of this retreat, I remember the quiet Austin mornings when these centering prayers were written. I cherish those years of interior growth and especially the community of spiritual friends who supported my flourishing.

My own prayer is that the words in this book nurture you beyond the written word into the womb of silence experienced through some method of receptive prayer, such as centering prayer or the Jesus prayer. They are shared here with the wish that they might nourish a deepening experience of God's love, especially when read as a prelude or postlude to periods of contemplative prayer.

The prayers are sent forth in printed form with the hope that they reach brothers and sisters of Spirit gazing across their own oceans of devotion. We are connected through word and silence, growing ever deeper in God's love.

PREFACE TO THE WOMEN'S EDITION

It is a joy to mark the ten-year anniversary of the first edition of *Centering Prayers,* with this new revised edition *for women.*

May these prayers be a kind of companion for you, wherever you might be on your spiritual journey. Whether you are a seasoned practitioner of deep contemplative prayer or brand new to prayer, I hope you will find herein a personally curated nourishing influence to begin each day, especially when paired with silence.

May each page be a kind face to you, where you can turn to speak and be spoken to—

> words to take you deeper into the heart of God's love,
>
> words to take you deeper into the presence of Spirit's care,
>
> and words to take you deeper into the silence.

And may it be that through these prayers, you, dear reader, may feel woven together with other unknown friends on the journey of faith. We are a community of human beings who are discovering together how much silence speaks to our hearts and helps our hearts speak to others.

With these wishes, I commend this book of prayers to you, and with hands pressed together at the heart, I bow to you, as a brother in Christ of the family of Mary, following Word and Wisdom into the golden quiet of God.

—Peter Traben Haas

"Quiet time alone, contemplation, prayer, music, a centering line of thought or reader, of study or work. It can be physical or intellectual or artistic, any creative life proceeding from oneself. It need not be an enormous project or a great work. But it should be something of one's own. Arranging a bowl of flowers in the morning can give a sense of quiet in a crowded day – like writing a poem, or saying a prayer. What matters is that one be for a time inwardly attentive. . . . Center-down, say the Quaker saints. To the possession of the self the way is inward, says Plotinus. The cell of self-knowledge is the stall in which the pilgrim must be reborn, says St. Catherine of Siena."

—Anne Morrow Lindbergh

"In prayer, we discover what we already have. You start where you are and you deepen what you already have and you realize you are already there. We already have everything, but we don't know it and we don't experience it. Everything has been given to us in Christ. All we need is to experience what we already possess."

—Thomas Merton

JANUARY

It is as if God says to us:

Your radiance cannot be hidden by your mistakes or by any external situation you may be experiencing.

Your life is hidden with me.

Rejoice a little today in this knowledge.

My love changes everything.

January 1
Seeds of intention

O God Who Calls Me into Life:

Standing on the strength of your everlasting foundation at the junction of a year completing and a year beginning, I cast forth my seeds of intention into the days unfolding before me this New Year.

Strengthened by the web of shared yet unseen hopes connected in silence, I see each choice as victory and the days to come as vibrant.

In Christ, it is and shall be.

Amen.

January 2
You are the One

Lord Jesus, Living Christ:

Empty, I am filled.

Heavy, I am carried.

Lost, I am guided.

Imprisoned, I am released.

Angry, I am calmed.

Anxious, I am given peace.

Alone, I am visited.

Hopeless, I am reminded of miracles.

Hungry, I am fed.

Thirsty, I am quenched.

On and on the reversals go—you are the One who turns my water into wine. You touch my life with your Word and say, "Be free. Be filled. Be light. Be found. Be peace. Be abundance. Be love. Be joy. Be life."

Amen.

January 3
Resting with you

God of my Beginnings:

For the soul that longs for God, the silence awaits.

For the heart that hungers for God, worship is calling.

I begin this year with the simplicity of silence.

Resting with you, I become myself again.

Amen.

January 4
Replace my fears with love

Loving God:

Replace my fears with love.

Where I fear lack, bring abundance.

Where I fear sickness, bring wholeness.

Where I fear others, bring reconciliation.

Where I fear being wrong, bring freedom.

Forgive the ways I use fear as an excuse to limit love.

Forgive me when I use my thoughts and words as tools of fear.

You are love.

Humanity is your beloved.

I often forget this in my fears. Today, I wish to remember.

Amen.

January 5

My name is greeted with the morning

God of New Life:

My name is greeted with the morning of a new year. I am invited into your presence of love to know myself in the embrace of others. Such communion is my first awakened song. And I celebrate.

Amen.

January 6
I remember your love

Loving God:

Like the ancient Magi, help me recognize and receive the divine presence in another.

Connected in this union of distinction, I remember your love that wishes to appear through me today as Epiphany.

Amen.

January 7
You welcome me into your rest

Loving God:

In all my movement, you are present.

When I am busy and burdened, you welcome me into your rest.

When I am cold and alone, you invite me into the warmth of your love.

While many ideas are available to humanity, when I am at rest, I discover that your living presence is beyond idea; it is experience.

I welcome this gift.

Amen.

January 8
Underneath every burden

Beloved of my Heart:

Underneath every burden I feel is a blessing.

Loosen with gentleness each emotional knot tied too tight in the tug-of-war of my emotions.

You are with me despite the tensions made tight by the living of life.

In your silent grace, I receive the gentleness to hold my questions with acceptance and my dreams with trust.

I affirm today that in Christ nothing can separate me from you—including my own thoughts and feelings.

Amen.

January 9
To feel your heart blazing

Home of My Heart:

God of all who worry and wander, draw me home to your heart.

In prayer, I wish to feel your heart blazing with a heat that holds everything together while fears seek to crack me apart.

In and through Jesus Christ, fire of my heart, fusion of loving fellowship, help of humankind.

Amen.

January 10
Bring wholeness

Source of My Strength:

Bring wholeness to the fragmentation of my thoughts, feelings, and actions.

Release my constrictions against others, myself, and your faithful love.

Set me free from my shames, healed through surrender into your ever-sustaining grace.

Amen.

January 11
You are the first light in the depths of the deep

God of Mercy:

You are the first light in the depths of the deep.

Draw me into the silence to feel your closeness and send me into the world attuned to the movement of your mercy, beyond the cultural swings of all or nothing, winning or losing, peace or conflict.

Amen.

January 12
Sealed with your strong, unflinching love

Beloved:

I take you for better or worse, richer or poorer, in sickness or in health, today and for all the days of this journey into your love.

Sealed with your strong, unflinching love, I am free to be present to the world and my responsibilities, assured that you are with me, and I am with you.

Amen.

January 13
Soften my edges as your grace forms me

O Lord, Giver of This Journey:

Soften my edges as your grace forms me.

Uncoil me by your incomprehensible love and grace.

How else shall I reply to such blessings than to kneel with adoration as you gift me with the inheritance of your healing Word?

Amen.

January 14
The unshakable silence of love

Abba:

Some days I remember I need more help than I realize.

Today, I surrender to your grace.

You are holding all who suffer with the unshakable silence of love.

Each moment is a gift received, each human a part of your whole.

In the name of Jesus Christ, who holds us all together in grace.

Amen.

January 15
My inner life grounded in you

Almighty God:

As life on this planet increasingly becomes tumultuous, I wish to have my inner life grounded in you through Christ by the Spirit.

I begin this day, consenting to your presence and action within.

Amen.

January 16
The strength of your love

Lord Jesus, Living Christ:

Strengthen me in love.

Nourish me in faith.

Draw me into your life.

I enter this day in the strength of your love.

Amen.

January 17
The power of mercy lifting my mind

Balm for the Broken Places:

Thank you for the gift of words that do their transforming work through the voices of prophets and martyrs of truth.

Thank you for the fierce mercy of nonviolent resistance in the face of shame, torture, and ignorance.

Thank you for the power of mercy lifting my mind beyond limited boundaries into the realm of deeper love and understanding, even amidst injustice.

I humbly offer my life as a continuation of the voice and work of truth—to birth more mercy in the face of cruelty and tears of sorrow.

Amen.

January 18
Let the kingdom of my heart open

Beloved Wisdom, Holy Compassion:

I wish to feel the touch of your blessing today in the empty places of my being.

Where you see there is lack of wisdom, love, or goodness, bring insight, compassion, and openheartedness.

Let the kingdom of my heart open and expand toward someone new today, releasing that which represses me in self-absorption.

Amen.

January 19
The miracle of your life in me

Spirit of God:

Move in my life. Unfold your growth in me, turn by turn in an open spiral woven into your love.

I am warmed inside by the miracle of your life in me.

Amen.

January 20

A vessel of adoration

Loving God:

Use every person and complexity to anoint me as a vessel of adoration, reflecting the light of love instead of perpetuating the frictions of personality.

Amen.

January 21

The inwardness of my being

Lord of Life:

I wish to feel invigorated today by your love that leads me into wholeness. Connect the current of your life with the inwardness of my being.

I wish to be well by connecting with you in my heart-center, receiving abundance to share it abundantly.

In and through Christ this can and shall be.

Amen.

January 22
Inside the silence

Lord God of All Creation:

In your grace, my wrong turns become unexpected paths.

Inside this grace, you enable my surrender, and there I find your love.

Inside your love, I find silence.

Inside the silence, you are, and I become.

Amen.

January 23
Make your love visible

Living Love:

Make your love visible through me in the exchange of my words and glances toward others. Help me see how every small, simple gesture and chore can also become a doorway to give and receive kindness and care.

Amen.

❋

January 24
Lifting my sorrows into joy

Holy Spirit:

Transform my private Scripture reading into your personal love with me in the inner chamber of my heart, lifting my sorrows into joy.

Turn on the lights of radiant wisdom in me through your life-giving Word.

Amen.

❋

January 25
At the center of all that lives

Abba:

I begin this day with gratitude for the gift that is hidden in my center.

Yet I also see that I hurt the very ones I wish to love.

Remind me in the silence that I am connected to you in Christ by more than what keeps me apart.

Help me see that at the center of all that lives is a small piece of the very beginning, which was with you and is now your Word always with us.

Amen.

January 26
In the shelter of your presence

Beloved:

Let me dwell in the shelter of your presence.

There is no end to my falling into your love, yet your love holds firm.

Life and all its situations will not shelter me.

Nor will my successes.

Therefore, today I make the inward turn to silence to feel your strength as the energy for all my doings and the calm for my deepest rest.

In Christ, soul of my soul, I pray.

Amen.

January 27
Lead me home

Most Merciful and Loving Abba:

Thank you for always hearing my heart as it rises up in prayer through Christ. Nurture in me today the awareness of your personal closeness.

I wish to grow in consciously chosen mercy and love, beyond my likes, dislikes, and opinions. In Christ, I hold others' perceptions in reverence.

When I fall back into forgetfulness and wander into judgment, lead me home to your loving embrace, which extends perfectly to all.

Amen.

January 28
Transform me into love

Lord God of Light and Love:

Awaken in me the desire for you.

Free me from the fears that cripple.

Connect me to the joy that brings freedom.

Transform me into love.

Open me to wisdom and live through me as the way, the truth, and the life.

Amen.

January 29
I live in the field of wholeness

O Path of Life, Journey of Love:

I live in the field of wholeness in which I can awaken and become aware that you wish to live through me.

I welcome the recognition that whatever is occurring is perfect for my transformation in Christ.

Amen.

January 30

In between, we learn to love

Sustainer of My Life:

Your love speaks in the middle of the night when I feel all alone.

Your love stays with me when no one else will.

Your love remembers when everyone else forgets.

Your love gives third chances, again and again.

Your love sees a life of beauty when others only see emotional baggage.

God is love.

We come from God.

We return to God.

In between, we learn to love.

All things come and go.

Love endures forever.

Amen.

January 31
Where I feel less than perfect

God of Unending Welcome:

Prompt my heart into honesty.

Where I feel mocked, inspire a connected courage that feels the oneness of human life beyond our differences.

Where I feel less than perfect, remind me that nothing can separate me from your love—including other people's judgments or my own doubts and fears.

This I pray through Christ, the one and the many.

Amen.

FEBRUARY

It is as if God says to us:

Whatever path of loneliness or loss you may be traveling, miracles of love and supply will arrive: your heart is beating; your lungs are breathing; your mind is bright with conscious light.

Beyond your thoughts of lack and longings for love is a truth of my reality: My love has always met and will always meet all your needs. The sea will part. The storm will calm. My presence changes everything.

But you must change your inner world of how you see things. And that is the secret to your freedom. The mind's eyes are the window to your soul. Perception is the path. Truth is the light that guides the way. If you wish a different path, cleanse your perception with my truth.

To change the way you take in impressions is to change your life. No one else can do this for you—including me. I give Truth. You are invited to put it to use. For this, my grace abounds.

February 1
Awaken me more into the realm of faith

Lord Jesus Christ:

Awaken me more into the realm of faith that I might feel your power working through me as a vessel of divine healing.

Let me be the conduit of your healing touch. Give me the courage in that moment to forget myself and simply remember you.

Amen.

February 2
Write your words deep in my heart

Abba:

As I dwell in the shelter of your love, I hope to become a participant of your unfolding story.

Write your words deep in my heart. Seal understanding and inner meaning in the chambers of my mind.

I wish to recognize wisdom, receive it, and dedicate my heart to its path.

In the temple of your truth, I believe in order to understand.

Amen.

February 3
You turn my failures into perfect love

God of Mercy:

You turn my failures into perfect love.

Help me remember this truth and to forget all things to the contrary.

I am not defined by the surface of things, or any flaws.

I am defined by the One from whom I came and to whom I return, and you, O God, are the essence of love and completion.

Amen.

February 4
Your hidden love

O Most Sacred Life of Christ:

Ground me in your hidden love.

Bloom me in your unbounded joy.

Amen.

February 5
Graceful centering in your silence

God of Perfect Provision:

Your truth feeds me on the journey to the banquet of your presence.

Bring me into the balance of being one with you through Christ by the Spirit, and through this graceful centering in your silence, feed the hunger and thirst you have placed within me.

Today, I wish to experience your love in the garden of your presence—and in the city of humankind.

Amen.

February 6
In your love I live

God of Resurrection Light:

In your love I live, and in your life, I am lifted out of the darkness and divisions of any shards of sorrow, into the beauty of your mirror of love.

Amen.

February 7
You are drawing me out of the shadows

God, Birther of the Heavens:

Today, I pray to deeply remember that you are drawing me out of the shadows and filling my heart with love. A song of prayer arises: When in darkness with no light but that which in my heart does burn, you, Lord Jesus Christ, bring the warmth of love.

Amen.

February 8

Recognize, receive, and remember your love

Eternal and Loving God:

Superficial life attempts to smother the truth that I am a chosen beneficiary of your love.

Help me remember today. Help me wake up more fully to it.

May I recognize, receive, and remember your love, despite any external evidence to the contrary.

Your love operates under a different set of rules that I don't fully comprehend. But I can feel your love healing me, and that makes all the difference.

Amen.

February 9
You are the space in between every breath

God Beyond Words and Understanding:

You are the silence underneath my waiting.

You are the space in between every breath, sob, shout of sorrow, grief, or desperation.

You are everything.

Draw me now into the inner heart of this life, knowing beyond knowing the gift of your presence.

Amen.

February 10
Even death holds my hand

God of My Life:

I am not just flesh and bones but living breath, rising into relationship and Son-song, worship, and service. My future is unveiled in the open tomb. Embraced by emptiness, I am fearless and assured that everything in life can become my teacher.

Even death holds my hand, instructing me in the way of my Master—risen, unconquerable light amidst the shadows.

I see death is a ripe fruit and flower of this lifetime.

Amen.

February 11
Cultivate in me a skillfulness to love

Source of My Being:

Stretch me beyond the demand for personal advantages.

Increase my capacity for silence. Diminish my negative reactivity.

Teach me the balanced way of holding life-tensions with hope.

Expand my tolerance for ambiguity and acceptance of others as they are, reducing my addiction to making others wrong.

Cultivate in me a skillfulness to love, using every situation and life experience as a means for growth toward your likeness.

Amen.

February 12
Perceive your presence

Lord Jesus Christ:

Show me the way to purity of heart.

Open my eyes to see beyond the senses. I wish to perceive your presence and participate in the experience of knowing reality.

Amen.

February 13
Transform the water of my life

Lord God of All Creation:

Transform the water of my life into the red wine of holy love.

Fashion this transformation in me and give me the courage to share what I have been given.

Amen.

February 14
Guard my heart

God My Beloved:

I belong to you.

Guard my heart. Increase my devotion.

Guide me through the whirlwind of daily chores and errands.

Use every task as a teacher and every activity as an opportunity to rest in your presence amidst the demands of the day.

Through it all, nourish me with your Word and flourish me in silence.

Amen.

February 15
Deepen my attention to silence

To the Living God I Pray:

Deepen my attention to silence at the center of this inward breath, drawing me beyond the surface of things into the heart of your Christ.

Let this occur in the midst of my commerce and movement, conversations and encounters.

I wish to truly awaken to my hidden vocation as a temple of your Spirit, becoming an embodied messenger of your love, grace, and goodness.

Amen.

February 16

Held through the sways of life by your grace

To the God Who Is Here I pray:

The fullness of your Word feeds me, transforming seeds of truth into miracles of love and joy.

In this moment, I feel and remember who I am. Help me live according to this deep-seated knowledge. I wish to feel held through the sways of life by your grace.

Amen.

February 17

Touched by the presence of your sustaining love

Beloved:

Pour out your Spirit upon me today so that my small suffering might be touched by the presence of your sustaining love.

Amen.

February 18
Your grace that connects

God My Center:

Throughout this day, bring your grace in the midst of aggravations to my spirit.

Help me remain in contact with your grace that connects all despite the attacks of words and gestures by others.

When I feel swamped by the frustrations and difficulties of life that seem personally against me, help me enter your kingdom of love, available always right here and now.

Amen.

February 19
The peace of mind to remain silent

God of Peace:

Between the extremes of hatred and love, bring peace into my relationships.

Lessen the pendulum swings of negative emotions in my body, mind, and emotions.

Where I am unable to say anything that nurtures love, give me the peace of mind to remain silent.

Through Christ, the Prince of Peace, I pray.

Amen.

February 20
The warmth of divine love

Holy Spirit of God:

Anoint me with the warmth of your divine love made visible in the exchange of words and glances.

Turn my curiosities of faith into a gentle cadence of devotion.

Amen.

February 21

The open–hearted surrender to grace

God My Center:

Your ever-increasing love is offered even through the upheavals of life. You hold the center as life spins, taking its turns from one generation to the next.

I listen in the silence for the peace that can't be understood or shaken. It is your life-giving word meeting me face to face in the open-hearted surrender to grace that each moment offers.

I begin this day saying yes to the strength of your center.

Amen.

February 22
Your loving presence enduring

God of Abraham and Sarah:

I give thanks for this day and the gift of life. While I may not understand why things are the way they are, I can feel your loving presence enduring even amidst my uncertainty, and so I pray:

Amidst temptations, give me the will to choose what is right.

In my hurry, give me patience to remain silent as I wait for wisdom.

When I am successful, give me gratitude to recognize how much I have been given.

Amen.

February 23
Deeper into Abba's love and Mary's example

Lord Jesus, Living Christ:

You returned good for evil, blessings for curses, love for hate, and acceptance for accusations.

You have shown me that the way to transformation is through surrender—giving up my will to power, success, and control.

Draw me into inner solitude and silence so that I might follow you deeper into Abba's love and Mary's example.

Amen.

February 24
Hold me close

Loving God:

Seal me from negative thoughts and feelings.

Neutralize this negativity lest it spread.

I wish to have my feeling of "I" in you and not in myself, my situations, or my turbulent moods that ebb and flow with life events.

Hold me close, in Word, Sacrament, Scripture, and silence.

Amen.

February 25
Toward the infinite vastness of Christ

O God, My Mother-Father:

I begin this day in the safety of your ever-present love.

Shift my attention away from just myself and toward the infinite vastness of Christ.

Amen.

February 26

I embrace my role as a reflection of your glory

Sophia Spirit:

My mind is a center for reception. Enlighten my every cell.

Give me the wisdom to see what needs to be said, done, and undone.

I embrace my role as a reflection of your glory. Imbue my countenance with the joyful inheritance I have been given as a co-heir with Christ.

Amen.

February 27
The deepest truth you are inviting me to remember

God of Transformation:

You call me into the heart to listen for your voice, ignoring the chatter of my mind. Help me to observe and not identify with the inner dialog, especially when it is negative and self-critical.

I wish to personally experience your Word feeding my ongoing transformation with truth and wisdom, revealing the deepest truth you are inviting me to remember.

Amen.

February 28
Where I end and you begin

Transforming Trinity:

Help me accept your invitation to live in you so deeply that I can't tell where I end, and you begin.

Amen.

February 29, leap year

Tune my heart

God Whose Name Is "I Am":

The becoming of the world needs me. Tune my heart into the calling that I uniquely am here to receive and embody.

Give inspiration for the days when I feel lost and uncertain how to contribute to the well-being of those I love.

Amen.

MARCH

It is as if God says to us:

I am the eternal waiting for all to return home to me.

Your arrival is not to a place per se.
It is to a relationship.

Your prayer supports your return and
our growing relationship.

March 1
I may not feel your grace right now

God Who Lifts Me Up:

Although I may not feel your grace right now.

Although I may be identified with negative feelings at this moment.

Nevertheless my failures and falls are trustworthy teachers.

You, O my God, are using all things so that in Christ you might be all in all.

Amen.

March 2
Certain you are here

O Lord My God:

Open to your love, I feel you teaching me today through the simple movements of my daily life and especially through my resting prayer in your presence.

Certain you are here, I trust that all things today will work together for my good.

Amen.

March 3
All is well

God of Tender Mercy:

Sometimes I am tempted to close down in fear and frustration. In that moment, I give thanks for your tender mercy assuring me that all is well. You are here.

Amen.

March 4
Finding abundant life

God Who Waits:

I return to the cave of my heart today, finding abundant life in you.

Resting there, I am awakened to the gift of my being and becoming in your presence.

I offer my being and becoming as a song of praise in the silence.

Amen.

March 5
Caught in the mystery of this life

God of Love and Light:

During these days may you—

Light the lamp of my eyes with wisdom.

Light the torch of my heart with love.

Cure my sadness.

Warm my coldness.

Drench my inner drought with your divine love.

Lead me into the abandonment of your loving embrace.

Caught in the mystery of this life, I am upheld by the experience of your love in the silence.

Through Christ, with Christ, in the unity of the Spirit.

Amen.

March 6

Set my heart to sail deeper into your love

Eternal and Loving God:

I am filled with a sweetness that rises into my heart with song. Perhaps it is the feeling of love. Ancient melodies remind me of an untold freedom, long lost, awaiting me. Shall I finally believe it and set my heart to sail deeper into your love?

Amen.

March 7

The only wound that need not ever heal

Abba:

Quicken in me the presence of your living Word, through whom I receive the wound of love so to ponder the beauty and grace of all things created.

Your wound humbles me to tears, not so much in pain, but in the joy of your mercy. This is the only wound that need not ever heal, whose symbol is the cross and whose image is your descending dove.

Amen.

March 8
What needs to be forgiven, healed, and celebrated

Giver of Life and Love:

Embrace me with mercy and grace. You know what is stored within my heart. You know what needs to be forgiven, healed, and celebrated. Speak to me in the silence and teach me in the light of your love.

Amen.

March 9
The uprising of your energy

God of Transformation:

Help me feel again the uprising of your energy meeting me in the furnace of my being.

May the fire of the Spirit burn away the layers of my falseness that cannot possibly work in the light of your love.

Amen.

March 10
Upheld in the light of your resurrection

Strength of My Life:

I am promised that there is a stream by which I may grow in every season, flowing with living water available for my flourishing if I drink it day and night. Yet, I am often hindered in doing so by distractions and undisciplined habits.

Sometimes it seems impossible such growth could ever happen in me.

Help me, Lord. I wish to walk with joy, upheld in the light of your resurrection.

Amen.

March 11
With me in suffering and shock

God My Father and Mother:

You are here with me in suffering and shock.

Have mercy and help.

As the world spins, draw my attention to your Word in the silence. And to your presence in the silence. And to your wholeness amidst all that feels shattered.

Your presence, my hope for every suffering.

Your resurrection power, my strength for every despair.

Amen.

March 12
The strength of your Spirit

God of My Lifetime:

Protect me from the temptations of the world and the errors of thinking I am disconnected from you and others.

Fill my heart and body with the strength of your Spirit and illumine my mind with the knowledge of the wisdom of Christ.

Amen.

March 13
Unlock the mystery of life

God of My Lifetime:

What is the formula to unlock the mystery of life?

I surrender the life I call my own and discover it anew as a sheer gift. I am therefore free from the need to hold on to this thing called my "self," released to live by faith.

Amen.

March 14
Your vision for my becoming

Silent Love, Source of Life:

Prompt me into your possibilities and strengthen me through failures.

I release all my thoughts and feelings of accusation and guilt and receive the gift of freedom in your long-suffering love.

I consent to your work of renovation and trust your vision for my becoming.

Amen.

March 15
Turn my Lazarus life into resurrection love

Heart of Love:

Turn my Lazarus life into resurrection love.

Use the failures of my best efforts as the locations of your transforming grace. In my powerlessness to do, draw me into deeper union with you.

Amen.

March 16
The ashen mark upon my forehead

Spirit of God:

The ashen mark upon my forehead, now washed clean, remains in my heart as a symbol of my emptiness and my need for you.

Hungry, I can be fed.

Empty, I can be filled.

Barren, I can give birth.

And what is feeding, filling, and birthing in me but the incarnation of love itself?

This is not a test.

This is the unyielding power of Jesus Christ birthing in me something new.

Amen.

March 17
Everything is useful for my transformation

Indwelling Presence:

With the confidence of your love and goodness, reveal my self-serving tendencies to free me to become truly generous in love. I consent to your interior healing today, assured that in Christ everything is useful for my transformation.

Amen.

March 18
Eternity lingers deeper

Beloved:

I wait. I pray. Give me strength to endure this Lenten fast and help me with the sneaky temptations I don't expect.

Underneath my hunger, the taste of eternity lingers deeper than any satisfaction food might provide.

Amen.

March 19
Healing grace to all enduring wounds

Creator and Healer:

Awaken me to make amends to those I have wronged. Bring your life-creating power to my broken relationships and your healing grace to all enduring wounds.

Amen.

March 20
Fear no longer holds me

Living Presence:

I am abandoned unto you.

You are my strength.

You are my foundation.

I call upon you and am helped.

Fear no longer holds me. You do.

And you are love.

Amen.

March 21
The shadow hope of resurrection cresting near

Divine Love, Silent Presence:

As I enter into the final days of Lent, descending with Jesus into the remembrance of his Passion past, I look ahead to the shadow hope of resurrection cresting near, beneath any crosses I bear.

Explanations and justifications all pale to the color of pain I see among humankind. Strangely, I am comforted seeing that your resurrection light also contains all the hues of the human condition, including the color of our tears, violence, and suffering.

Amen.

March 22
Prepare me to be with you

Lord Jesus, Living Christ:

Prepare me to be with you in the center of Jerusalem in my worshipful heart. Gather me in the upper room of my mind to meet with you in devotion and friendship.

I am ready to receive you. I steel my heart to stand in wonder as you surrender to the violent depths of the human condition for my rescue and healing.

Amen.

March 23
Turn my demands into preferences

O God My Healer:

Turn my demands into preferences,

and my preferences into detachment,

and detachment into pure love,

and love into union,

consummating into only oneness so that there is no other—

to be judged, demanded, preferred, or even loved.

Amen.

March 24
A bad case of the human condition

Holy Spirit:

Your quiet fire purifies me to the depths with a subtle love.

It is so powerful I begin to recognize that I have come from you at the same time I become aware I have strayed, spending energy pursuing programs for my own happiness rather than listening to your love.

I confess I have a bad case of the human condition. But you have the perfect remedy.

In the silence, your healing unfolds, one layer after another, until Christ is unbound and revealed risen in and through me and all who cry out for help in simple faith.

Amen.

March 25

Release my demands for my life to be different

Jesus Christ, My Life:

You have shown me the way of surrender.

Help me release my demands for my life to be different. In total gratitude, I wish to accept life as it occurs today, neither thinking I deserve more nor feeling guilty for all I have been given.

I rest in humility recognizing that all things work together for my transformation in and through you.

Amen.

March 26

The swift light of conscious love

Lord Jesus, Living Christ:

May the swift light of conscious love lift my life through any weariness loading me down.

May the lightness of your love uphold me amidst any sinking feelings of guilt, shame, or depression.

May the wind of grace soar me over any dead-end choices that lead nowhere.

Amen.

March 27
Sometimes silence is saying enough

Radiating Light, Unbounded Love:

I wish to speak of my gratitude, yet I cannot say what I wish to say.

Your love overwhelms me.

Sometimes silence is saying enough.

In and through Christ I live, move, and have all my saying and unsaying.

Amen.

March 28
The way into the mystery

God of Peace:

Grant me the grace to meet each thing, event, and relationship I perceive as a problem today with a deepened attention to the center that holds all things together with an intelligence that transcends my perceptions.

Where I feel friction with others, reveal the way into the mystery of seeing how your love connects the many ways of being and the multiple points of human perspective, all with perfect harmony.

Amen.

March 29
Gift me with faithful companions

Holy Spirit:

Draw me to you. And draw others to me.

Gift me with faithful companions who support my intentions to follow the way despite the competing allurements and alternative paths and programs for happiness that tempt me to neglect my deepest intentions to tend and befriend.

Amen.

March 30
Your Word is the occurrence of total self-giving love

Holy Spirit of God:

Beyond comparison, beyond despair, beyond every heart, mind, and body care, your guiding, encircling love connects me to the truth so easily hidden by structures of power, control, and wealth.

The truth is that this world emanates from your Word and your Word is the occurrence of total self-giving love.

Amen.

March 31
A world in process of being reborn

Living and Radiant Source of Love:

Awaken me to the importance of wisely using my time to prepare a reservoir of interior peace.

Show me how to identify with common human difficulties through fasting, prayer, and almsgiving and to realize that my own problems do not define me but can connect me through empathy to a world in the process of being reborn.

Amen.

APRIL

It is as if God says to us:

With simple acceptance of my Triune mystery, join with the community of saints to remember my promises.

During this month of new life through death, please know, feel, and remember how hope comes close in the depths, bringing my Son's light, life, and love.

April 1

You are the shadow that crosses near in the silence

Living God:

You are the center of the cosmos and the summation of all that has ever been said.

You are the awakening that warms the world.

You are the living connection holding me close in my seasons of separation.

You are the source of oneness binding the earth and its people to our unseen foundation and emerging destiny.

You are the shadow that crosses near in the silence of prayer.

Amen.

April 2
To the depths of outer darkness

Lord Jesus:

You who went all the way down into the human condition and beyond to the depths of outer darkness can return and rescue me all the way up to God and the heights of eternal light. This is the moment the word *hallelujah* was born.

Amen.

April 3
The chalice of your silent love

O God Beyond My Comprehension:

I drink the water of liquid faith, poured from the chalice of your silent love. My secret name is etched forever in the book of life, and I receive this heralded victory like a promise of love sealed with your Gethsemane tears.

Amen.

April 4
A more complete child of God

Beloved Jesus Christ:

Under your mercy, failures become my best teacher, showing me how to live more freely in your love. Through your resurrection, ward off the harmful influences and experiences of life.

Give your living water and bread of life so that I may become a more complete child of God, not just a servant of life.

Amen.

April 5
Soften the preferences that separate

Beloved Source of Life:

I wish to feel your risen power in the center of my heart. Let this Easter season be for melting my inner ice blocks into living water. Soften the preferences that separate and draw me into the love that unites.

In this practical work, I am held by Christ, whose cross and tomb are symbols of your invitation to a different kind of life. I choose to surrender self so as to receive resurrection to life.

Amen.

April 6

Transform my patterns of judgment

Heavenly Father:

Transform my patterns of judgment into abounding grace. Heal the pain in me that restricts the freedom of your love and of Christ's resurrection. Let me eat the fruit of peace.

Amen.

April 7
Asking, seeking, and knocking

Divine Healer:

I'm asking, seeking, and knocking to know and experience more of your will for my life and the power of your right-now-ever-sustaining love.

Amen.

April 8
A temple of truth

Beloved:

Teach me the truth of your reality in my ordinary experiences. I consent to your point of view and wish to cease being my own fixed point of reference.

You are the life I long for yet resist in my attempts to find life everywhere else. Gently transform me into a temple of truth in union with Jesus Christ by the power of your Holy Spirit.

Amen.

April 9
Hold me while I grow

Abba:

Open me with the gentleness of your love.

I see that I have room to grow and request the insights necessary to surrender more completely even without complete understanding.

You are bringing about in me something more than I can ask or imagine. Give me patience as you hold me while I grow.

I affirm that your presence is sufficient for all situations that I encounter on this unfolding journey.

Amen.

April 10
My deepest truth in the face of life's deepest darkness

Lord Jesus, Living Christ:

You are the answer to my deepest questions.

You are my stability in all my uncertainty.

You are provision to all my needs.

Your love dwells with me in the temple of my heart and mind.

In you, there is nothing that can separate me from God.

With these prayerful intentions, I declare my deepest truth in the face of life's deepest darkness. I challenge the shadows of doubt, depression, anger, fear, and judgment with the light of resurrection love.

Amen.

April 11
Depths of your life and heights of your love

Living God of Life and Love:

I aim to order my days by the inner awareness of heaven and my moments by the in-breath of Spirit through Word and sacrament.

Reveal the mystery of Christ to me in personal and profound ways.

Let heaven's highest level of feeling and thinking occur in me, to see the depths of your life and heights of your love beyond my judgments, perceptions, and false-self motivations.

Amen.

April 12
Your abundance of grace

Lord Jesus, Living Christ:

Your multi-chance love extends deeper than all my bareness and failures. It extends, over and again, as practical grace uplifting, helping, sustaining, providing in every moment of my life.

Just when I thought I could not or do not have what it will take, you invite me to trust you and cast my net into your abundance of grace.

Amen.

April 13
Defined by your love

Heart of My Heart:

Remind me again in the silence of prayerful surrender that I cannot explain my own existence. Life is a gift.

I am not defined by my situations. I am defined by your love. Enlarge me for prayer. Just because I can't see the stars in the daylight does not mean they are not there. I am like that; always in you and you in me, despite appearances in life to the contrary.

Today, I remember: Christ in me, the hope of glory.

Amen.

April 14
Through the places of my brokenness

Ministering Spirit of God:

Help me remember that I come from you and return to you, and in between I am invited to grow in love. I wish to feel your grace attending to me through the places of my brokenness, inviting me deeper into your love.

Amen.

April 15
Deepen my understanding

Abba:

Deepen my understanding so that I do not drift in the mist of doubt or miss the mark of your living truth. Bring me to new life in an ever-flourishing relationship with your Son, my shepherd, Jesus Christ.

Amen.

April 16
Thank you

Most Holy and Loving God:

Thank you today for the gift of life.

Thank you for awakening me to your abundant life.

Help me to see you amidst all my day-to-day living.

Amen.

April 17
Startle me with your beauty and goodness

Lord Jesus, Living Christ:

As I begin a new day in this Resurrection season, I request an attentive heart. Despite the busy days, help me to stop and listen for your movements. Startle me with your beauty and goodness hiding in plain sight.

Amen.

April 18
Deepen my spiritual friendships

Holy Trinity of Light, Life, and Love:

Draw me into spiritual community with you and with others. Deepen my spiritual friendships and draw me amongst brighter beings in whose company I might feel understood and whose common aims and interests will be a help to my journey.

I recognize and request this need for my own life and agree to try and do the same in the lives of others where needed. Respond and surprise me with your provision.

Amen.

April 19
Support my intentions

Holy Spirit:

Draw me to you on this one-way journey to the heart of our Father in Christ the Son.

Gift me with faithful companions who support my intentions to follow this way despite all the competing allurements and alternative paths promising happiness.

Amen.

April 20
Release me from my personal agendas

Lord Jesus:

Gently release me from my personal agendas and impulsive actions so that I might live more completely under the certainty of your leading, guiding, and teaching.

As you do, fill my heart with lighthearted joy, raising me up from the heaviness of gloom.

Amen.

April 21
Your love in me and my life in you

Abba:

I rest in your continued anointing.

Guide my intellect to clearly see.

Guide my will to harmoniously choose.

Open my heart to feel your love in me and my life in you.

Amen.

April 22
I am part of this living Word from the beginning

Source of All Life:

Your Word sustains all life and brings order amidst the chaos. I am part of this living Word from the beginning. Today, I say "yes" to your wish for the flourishing of the creation. Through prayer and action, I agree to play my part so that the will of heaven may be more present here on earth.
Amen.

April 23
I cast myself upon your goodness

Beloved of My Heart:

Today, I cast myself upon your goodness.

Words fail to describe the joy of my salvation.

You meet me in my despair.

You heal me in my brokenness.

You anoint me in my surrender.
Amen.

April 24
The healing my body needs

God My Healer:

In my certainty that you can bring the healing my body needs to become the fullness of what is possible as a co-heir with Christ, I surrender to you.

Amen.

April 25
The path I am to take

Threefold Holy One:

I try to pass courageously through life situations, challenges, temptations, and conflicts, requesting wisdom to make decisions according to the inspiration of your self-giving love, rather than the constrictions of my demands.

Reveal in clear ways the path I am to take today. Help me stay open to your love and awake to your presence in each person and every situation I encounter.

Amen.

April 26

You are the miracle

Lord Jesus, Eternal Christ:

I request for my life and for my beloveds:

forgiveness of every debt,

provision for every need,

strength for every weakness,

comfort for every trouble,

healing for every sickness,

peace for every anxiety,

joy for every sorrow,

presence for every absence,

bread for every hunger,

water for every thirst,

shelter for every storm.

You are the miracle. I await your whisper in the silence and envision your Word breathing these miracles to life.

Amen.

April 27
That my words may be life-giving

Lord Jesus, Living Christ:

Speak into my Lazarus life and unbind the love waiting to be born in me. Radiate your life into my heart that my words may be life-giving and my countenance joy-reflecting.

Amen.

April 28
Your house of wisdom

Spirit of Truth and Goodness:

The wisdom of God is infinite and unfathomable,
yet it becomes utterly personal when I ask for help.
I surrender to you the impulses to live by my own wisdom. In this quiet moment, I request that your house of wisdom might be opened to me more today than before.

Amen.

April 29
Your very name is a treatment

Holy One:

Your very name is a treatment for my body and soul. I speak it softly as my affirmation of your healing help in the spaces of my life.

Your name is a shield of light, wisdom itself blazing in the darkness.

Your name is a song of love wooing me into heartfulness and the possibilities of harmony.

Your name is a blue spring morning triumphing with the power of new life made green through the darkness.

I search my heart and find the silence and the Spirit who teaches me to say, "Hallowed be thy name."

Amen.

April 30

Loosen the webs

Almighty God:

Loosen the webs that entangle my heart and prevent the reception of your faithful love.

Prepare my life for the fullness of your presence.

Renewed through prayer today, I let go into the vastness of your depths and the vitality of your Word.

Amen.

MAY

It is as if God says to us:

This moment, right now, is alive with the possibility to surrender to my salvation. I can free you to live in love toward all, even when you are tempted to respond with less than love, forgiveness, or kindness.

With the full bloom of spring, remember that I wish for your flourishing. I invite you into fruitfulness in every relationship, and especially with me. I am with you, helping you to always reach an inner abundance, especially now.

May 1
Hold me in your steadfast love

Faithful Giver of Life:

Let your face shine on me.

Hold me in your steadfast love.

Let me know your forgiveness, for I call upon you. Let all my fears be cast out.

Let me speak with the integrity of truth.

Amen.

May 2
Pour out your Spirit

Divine Love:

Pour out your Spirit upon me that I might know and experience your presence, so that even on my worst day I have the certitude that you are bringing about my intended destiny.

Amen.

May 3
Keep me aware

Spirit of God:

Guide my choices today so that what I say and do corresponds to the truth of my union in Christ with you. While I go about my duties of the day, keep me aware and connected to the hidden source of your love, claiming me as a beloved despite my fickle faith.

Amen.

May 4
Your presence undergirding

Lord Jesus Christ:

Speak to me in the strength of your love so that I might surrender more of myself to you and recognize your presence undergirding every dimension and moment of my life.

Forgive my attempts to take control and live as if you are not ultimate reality bringing blessings beyond my limited perception.

Thank you for the inability to explain my own existence. Help me see how the suffering of this life is just the right place for me to surrender to your strength that holds all things together.

Amen.

May 5

The power to change everything

God of Perfect Provision:

For every fear I have of not being recognized, and for every hope I fear will not be fulfilled, remind me that you bring about unexpected gifts with the power to change everything and bless me beyond what I could ever ask or imagine.

Amen.

May 6
The rhythm of rest

God of Perfect Peace:

Give me the patience to wait for your best gifts in a world moving fast.

Draw me into the rhythm of rest that my body needs and the goodness of relationships that my heart craves.

While the world is unpredictable, reveal your life-giving presence permanently available in the silence.

Amen.

May 7
When I feel tempted

Ever Faithful One:

When I feel tempted to give up on love, please restore, replenish, encourage, uphold, sustain, empower, and provide all that is required for me to endure.

Amen.

May 8

The moment I was born

Everlasting Giver of Life:

There is a truth in me that shines despite its hiddenness. This truth was given the moment I was born. It is my identity, which comes from you. Whatever my boss or colleagues or family members or spouse or friends think they see when they look at me, there is more.

I stand in the knowledge of my deepest being today, with perfect assurance that nothing can separate me from your love in Christ.

Amen.

May 9
To simply be

Beloved:

Free me from the compulsion to do, get, or keep up appearances. Give me the courage to simply be and belong to you. Help me see your path to freedom when I am tempted to buy my way to what I think is happiness. Fill me again with the joys of life in Christ.

Amen.

May 10
Sustaining comfort

Lord Jesus, Living Christ:

Touch me with the sustaining comfort necessary to thrive throughout the demands of this day. Seal me from overreactions that deplete my force for love and fill me with the insights for dealing with difficult decisions and perplexing relationships.

Amen.

May 11
You are the gift

Spirit of God:

You are the gift my soul has been waiting for in the silence and throughout all the seasons of my life—even when I didn't know it.

Plant your Word in my heart and birth your wisdom through me in ways I can't begin to comprehend, to bless others through counsel, friendship, and a joyful countenance.

Amen.

May 12
I will surrender to silence

Creator and Life Giver:

I celebrate the drenching of your Spirit for the destiny of love and begin today saying "yes" to you, stepping back from myself to create a space for your grace to fill.

I will surrender to silence and consent to your holy presence and action.

Through this time of simple prayer, continue to transform my body into a temple of your light, life, and love.

Amen.

May 13
Nurture wholeness

Most Gracious and Loving God:

As I rest with you in prayer, I request the mind of Christ. Guide my decisions. Instruct my conversations. Nurture wholeness in my relationships.

In this moment, fill me with the awareness that in Christ by your Spirit I belong to you.

Amen.

May 14

Sink deeply into the silence

Beloved:

I wish to sink deeply into the silence and receive your life-giving rest.

For all demands upon me, for all the people who need my time and attention, for all the situations that require my best efforts, I request help.

Thank you for the ways your grace releases me from having to perform and liberates me to live freely in each moment—gently, lightly, calmly.

Amen.

May 15
Remind me

Lord Jesus Christ:

Anoint me with your Spirit so I can speak in love and act in truth.

Where I lack clarity, reveal your will.

Where I presume to know, teach me simple trust.

Where I am impatient, remind me of your timelessness.

Amen.

May 16
The impossible is possible

Lord Jesus, Living Christ:

In your grace the impossible is possible.

Awaken me to see this truth more clearly, especially when I am tempted to forget and believe the lie that everything depends upon me.

Amen.

May 17
Mercy nourishing growth

Abba:

I often taste the bitterness of judgment and criticism. Help me to feel my innocence in your mercy. Replace my narratives of blame, guilt, and shame with a melody of forgiveness.

Then, loosen the knots of judgment I tie around others, so that I too might forgive and feel your mercy nourishing growth.

Amen.

May 18
The everlasting highway of saints

Love Beyond All Love:

By your mercy, I am here on earth to receive and reflect your glory as a vessel of Christ.

By your grace, I am one mile of the everlasting highway of saints encircled in the light of prayer and worship destined for the city of God.

Amen.

May 19
To become love

Life-giving Trinity:

Thank you for the gift of the human journey.

Help me use this lifetime to become love.

Amen.

May 20
Connected to the reality of your love

Sky-Rending Fire of Love:

Everything I am experiencing today is connected to the reality of your love, even if I can't figure out how.

May the realm of your Spirit continuously uphold the destiny of humankind and lead me to personally experience and receive more fully the reality of Jesus Christ in sacrament and silence.

Amen.

May 21
The calm whisper of your Spirit

Light upon Light:

Since I do not know what this day will bring, I ask for indications of providence and guidance for my spiritual journey.

Open the ear of my soul to hear the calm whisper of your Spirit speaking directly to my heart and to believe again the ancient promises from above.

Open the eyes of my heart to see with the certainty of faith in the light of your loving purpose.

Amen.

May 22
Unveil my falseness with your love

Lord Jesus My Teacher:

You are my teacher. Unveil my falseness with your love. Help me see that there is nothing I need to hide from you. Heal the intentions of my heart so I can love and serve with freedom and generosity.

Amen.

May 23
See beyond the surface

Living God of Life and Love:

Help me see beyond the surface of my external judgments, superficial perceptions, and selfish motivations.

Turn me more into love.

Amen.

May 24
Your graceful way among us

Lord of the Universe:

I lift my voice in prayer with the chorus of the cosmos, grateful to be here witnessing your graceful way among us.

Your name is sung in praise by light.

May your wisdom flourish here on earth.

Amen.

May 25
The solitude of my prayer

Eternal Stillness, Expanding Love:

Speak to my heart in the silence and let your Word take shape in the solitude of my prayer, bringing increased joy and peace in my social interactions today.

Amen.

May 26
Your Spirit loves to work in the secret places of shame

God of Hope Who Moves Beyond Human Limits:

Give me strength to come face to face with the failure of my false ways. Jolt me with a vision of what my future can be in you.

Your Spirit loves to work in the secret places of shame and with my wounded memories accumulated over a lifetime.

Therefore, I ask for a quality of life manifesting the stability of wisdom and the fecundity of love.

In the name that is the highest power, my greatest joy, my deepest truth, and my strongest hope: the savior anointed, Jesus the Christ.

Amen.

May 27
Draw me into your depth

Abba:

Empower me today with a renewed force of will to know the fullness of your truth available to humankind.

I wish to feel the guidance of higher influences awakening me to your presence. Shepherd me beyond the fears of my surface personality and the demands of worldly interactions.

Draw me into your depth, which is also the height and breadth of the knowledge of your love in Christ.

Amen.

May 28
You write new stories with old sentences

Unending Word of Life:

You write new stories with old sentences.

You transform deep hurts into sources of love.

You are the one I seek in all my pursuits.

Hold me as I weep, and whisper strength when everything seems to be falling apart.

You are here with me.

In this moment, that is more than enough.

Amen.

May 29
Deepen this ancient belonging

Holy Spirit of God:

Connect me to the growing source that keeps me strong even when my body feels weak.

Nurture me through the flow of wisdom descending upon me over the years from lessons learned and passages read.

And I will praise you this day for the ways your playfulness keeps me grounded, your wisdom keeps me focused, and your intention keeps me moving into the mystery of your love for others. Deepen this ancient belonging and take me into eternity.

Amen.

May 30
Start in me

O God, My God:

Do not forsake your world and its nations.

May your Spirit of peace bring an end to all violence and war.

Start in me.

Amen.

May 31
Stimulate my sense of wonder

God of Creation:

Stimulate my sense of wonder to marvel at the existence of the universe and my place in it as a spiritual being in development through this embodied experience.

Help me feel your transforming and available love coming down through the ray of creation, calling me to more harmonious ways of thinking, feeling, and doing.

Amen.

JUNE

It is as if God says to us:

My love moves with the cadence of the earth, waltzing around the sun.

Soon I am bringing the light to full, to remind you how I am also the light of the world.

Watch for me. I will shine into your life with love.

June 1
Awaken me with your gentle light

Abba:

Pour out your Spirit upon my broken dreams and awaken me with your gentle light of love into the realization of your presence in my life today.

Amen.

June 2
Your connecting presence everywhere

Transforming Presence:

Come into me in the silence of prayer so I might perceive, relate, and respond to you, to myself, to others, and to the creation with increasing awareness to your connecting presence everywhere through Christ by the Spirit.

Amen.

June 3
More fully share in your life

Abba:

Lead me into the living water of Scripture and replenish me with your written Word so that I may more fully share in your life with peace, wisdom, and mindfulness.

Amen.

June 4
I request the transforming grace

Source of the Creation:

Incongruency is occurring on this planet between reality and the ideal. I am indeed fallen from the peace of paradise.

Today I request the transforming grace that spans the space between what is and what might be. May I play my part well in the power of your Holy Spirit.

Amen.

June 5

I turn my heart toward your resurrection

Beloved:

I enter into silence each morning and night like a spider spins its web by the light, catching nourishment in the solitude of its spindle threads.

I turn my heart toward your resurrection like the sunflowers spinning their golden heads to drink the light of day. It seems life is more alive on these June mornings as summertime unleashes its impulse to thrive.

My heart joins with the greening forest wondering what fruition will appear. What can the light of your love do in me?

I wait for you in the secret and safe silence. Your presence is like a dew upon my heart.

You've been here all along, hidden by the turning horizon now revealing your life in me.

Amen.

June 6
Taste this

Living God:

Your Spirit arrives as a morning rain, showing up like a surprise guest. Listening to her voice at my heart's doorway, I discover her name is loving-kindness.

She reaches toward me, cupped hands tending holy water. "I can heal you," she says, strength itself looking into my eyes.

"See, taste this. . . ." And I drink till overflowing.

Amen.

June 7
You are the key that unlocks the mystery

Lord Jesus Christ:

You are the key that unlocks the mystery of existence.

You are the Word that speaks through the silence.

You are the presence that attends to even imperfect me.

You are the life that vivifies the planet in the blood and bread of common things.

You are the one and the many in whom I return to the Beloved, existence itself in loving communion with all beings and becomings.

Amen.

June 8

The presence of your healing love

God of My Prayers:

Bless me with the presence of your healing love felt in the silence of my inner room.

I feel you calling to me. It's as if you are saying to my heart, "I wish to speak face to face with you in silent, wordless wonder."

Why do I resist?

O silent love, I consent to your Triune threefold presence, beloved creator, redeemer, and sustainer.

Amen.

June 9
The power of your protection

God of My Life:

Flow through my body today that I might know the joy of your creating.

The certainty of your presence.

The power of your protection.

And the fullness of your joy.

Amen.

June 10
Breaking the bonds of suffering

Beloved Beyond Boundaries:

I lift my heart in care for the poor, the kidnapped, the forsaken, the alone, the tortured, the abused, the hospitalized, the falsely accused, the hungry, the wounded souls of our world.

In the prayer of my heart, I request a different future, breaking the bonds of suffering, bringing healing and wholeness in the name of Christ.

Amen.

June 11
Your grace works

Abba:

Your presence underneath the noise of the demands of daily life fills my heart with peace.

Your Word cleanses negative emotions that I don't know how to stop on my own.

Your grace works in my inner room of silent prayer, taking away jealousies, hatreds, vanities, pride, and prejudices that hinder consciously chosen love.

Thank you for your healing grace.

Amen.

June 12
You hold me while I grow

Beloved Source of Security:

I wish for total freedom from all forms of destructive fear.

In its place, lead me into the freedom of surrender.

You hold me while I grow, and in this confidence, I release anxieties about my life, and trust you with my unfolding yet-to-be-written story.

Amen.

June 13
Worthy of love

Beloved Source of Love:

Assure me in the depth of my being just how worthy of love I am on your generous terms.

Renew my thinking in the light of this truth, so that all my actions are guided by a sense of contentment, not envy.

Amen.

June 14
Lead me deeper

Beloved One in Three:

Lead me deeper into the mystery of your love.

Help me feel your presence in my weaknesses and all my wonderings.

Amen.

June 15
Who I may become in your grace

Giver of Every Good Gift:

Help me see who I truly am beneath the masks of my making, and who I may become in your grace.

I pray in your most holy threefold name: Father, Son, and Holy Spirit.

Amen.

June 16

Make me meek in the shadow of your glory

God of Gentle Power:

Make me meek in the shadow of your glory, to better reflect your love and truth. Help me remember that I live and move and have my being in Christ.

Amen.

June 17

Fill my poverty with your completeness

Heart of My Heart:

Let me see you.

Let me feel you.

Let me know you.

Let me love you.

Fill my poverty with your completeness.

Satisfy my hunger and thirst with your integrating truth that leads to life.

Amen.

June 18

A school of love

Spirit of Christ:

Thank you for this day and for every opportunity I have and will experience. I wish it all for my development in being and growth in love, goodness, and wisdom.

Mediate each misunderstanding I experience with another that my relationships may become a school of love.

Amen.

June 19

You are my center and source

Living Presence, Silent Love:

I wait for your first move in the darkness of surrender, lifting me into joy.

Whatever else may happen today, you are my center and source, blinding light, burning love, blooming life.

Amen.

June 20
The awareness needed to choose the highest good

Spirit of God:

Activate in me the awareness needed to choose the highest good and to avoid that which leads to suffering, for my own life or for anyone else.

Amen.

June 21
Fill me with your living Word of love

Abba:

On this day in celebration of the fullness of sunlight, anoint me with your peace so that I might become a peacemaker.

Fill me with your living Word of love so that I might decrease in judgment and increase in care and kindness.

Amen.

June 22
Your leading in the silence

Living God of Love:

Give me ears to hear your request beneath the demands of this moment.

I wish to listen for your leading in the silence.

Help me listen beyond the stories I spin about others and my own self. Your leading is clear in the silence: "Love one another because you are one in me."

Amen.

June 23
The joy that can only arrive through love

Beloved Jesus Christ:

Pour out your Spirit upon me so I can more completely love my family. Strengthen me to work for the freedom that can only come through forgiveness and the joy that can only arrive through love.

Amen.

June 24
Inspire me with your spiritual love

Beloved Mother of Jesus:

You were the first to feel the heartbeat of Christ within.

Inspire me with your spiritual love so that I might be released more from my fragmentation into the freedom of wholeness in Christ.

Amen.

June 25
Love saturates the empty space

You Who Dwell in the Temple of My Heart:

Sweeten me in the silence as your Word of love saturates the empty space between the thoughts where grace can grow with speed and strength.

Do the one thing necessary in me that can't be undone by life or luck.

Make me more yours than my own until all there is, is Christ.

Amen.

June 26

Abide with me even while all of life is occurring

Lord Jesus Christ:

Awaken me by the touch of your Spirit to the presence of your closeness in each moment of my life.

Give me the courage I need to do what I have been asked to do.

Show me how to separate from the fearful thoughts and feelings that occur in response to all of life's demands.

Draw me deeper into your love and abide with me even while all of life is occurring.

Amen.

June 27
The miracle of many voices becoming one

Jesus Christ:

Refresh me by your Spirit.

Lead me into peace and understanding with others and help me experience the miracle of many voices becoming one in you.

Amen.

June 28
Strengthen and sustain me

Almighty God:

May the healing power flowing from the fountain-heart of Jesus Christ strengthen and sustain me with every consolation by his Word and Spirit.

Amen.

June 29
Let me hear the sacred names of God

Silent Giver of Life:

Let me hear the sacred names of God in the firmament of silence surrounding the earth and cosmos, from before time in the wordless Word that forms my being and all things.

You are made visible in the flourish of petals glowing orange in mid-summer heat; in the trickle of glacier melt watering the steep slopes, birthing life downstream.

O God, I name your wordless name in handfuls of this living earth, holy and bound to you from deep seas to high mountain heaps.

I name to revere, not conquer; to cherish, not exploit. Named in me, in you, in him and her, in this and that, in all things poured out to pour back to you.

Amen.

June 30
The joyful release of feeling forgiven

God of Joy:

To you, my Good Shepherd, I give my most basic self and all inner shadows that rise in opposition to love.

Use this day as my teacher.

Reveal where there is interior resistance to your truth and transformation and bring the joyful release of feeling forgiven in each moment when I remember who I am and what you wish for me to become.

Amen.

JULY

It is as if God says to us:

You are a lamp and my love is your fuel.

I love you and wish to anoint your life with the kind of light that heals your deepest darkness.

I am with you on your journey.

Follow the Light who knows the way
and is always close.

July 1
Give me the grace

Beloved Giver of Life:

When thoughts occur that lead to discouragement, give me the grace to not believe my own negativity.

Let the mind of Christ fill my thinking with praise, gratitude, and joy.

Amen.

July 2
Where miracles occur

Abba:

Lead me into the abiding place where miracles occur in the silence of your love, beyond all understanding.

Amen.

July 3
The encompassing of God

God Who Embraces Me:

The encompassing of God be upon my form and upon my frame.

The encompassing of divine love and grace be upon me eternally, shielding me from hate, from harm, and from all ill.

Amen.

July 4
Reveal the way of gentle love

God Beyond All Descriptions:

Show me the path through my pride and reveal the way of gentle love when I feel inflated with self-admiration.

Teach me Christ, who is the way, the truth, and the life, and my destination.

Amen.

July 5
You are already here

God of Perfect Holiness and Love:

Pour out your Spirit upon me and complete the renovation of my heart into a mansion of love.

I am an ordinary peasant waking each morning looking for bread.

I know that there is nowhere I need to go, for you are already here.

I see that there is nothing I need, for you have already given me everything by giving me yourself.

Amen.

July 6
Surprise me

Lord Jesus, Living Christ:

I wish to hear and feel your voice of love descending upon me in the movement of sunrise and the stillness of silence.

When I cannot see or recognize you in the form and field of my day-to-day vision, surprise me with the miracle of faith and joyful certitude.

Amen.

July 7
Speak my name in silence

Lord Jesus, Risen Christ:

As I face the presence of pain and suffering in my life, speak my name in silence. Even in the unknowing, I feel your presence.

Amen.

July 8
May your grace flow

I offer myself this day as a location through which your love can flow.

Let it be in me according to your Word.

May your grace flow in and through me today.

Amen.

July 9
Your presence changes everything

Beloved of my Life:

Nourish me with your love so that whatever is occurring in this life might be received with gratitude, recognizing that your presence changes everything.

Amen.

July 10

Help me listen

God of Mercy and Grace:

Facing the burdens of this day, help me listen for the Spirit song that rises on the periphery of my attention, reminding me of your constant provision and invitation to not worry about tomorrow.

Today is enough. Nurture in me the peace of silence so as to sing my own song.

Amen.

July 11

Turn my Martha worries into Mary peace

God Who Gives New Life:

Bless my journey as you turn my Martha worries into Mary peace. Harmonize my inner conflicts and place your hand of healing upon my interior life.

Amen.

July 12
Redefine my visions of success

Jesus, Servant of All:

Through faith, I ask your help to redefine my visions of success in the light of your total defeat through which the most unlikely of victories arose.

Amen.

July 13
Love the giver

Life-giving Love:

Whatever life may bring my way, you are what I am looking for.

Help me love the giver as much as I love the giver's gifts.

Amen.

July 14
Unveil your closeness

Eternal Listener:

Unveil your closeness by Word and Spirit.

Lead me deeper into your welcome body, soul, and mind.

Amen.

July 15
Welcoming what is

Most Gracious and Loving Heavenly Father:

My heart rests in the peace of surrender, welcoming what is and aspiring to what may be, in and through your grace and faithful love.

Amen.

July 16
The way of simplicity and surrender

Beloved Spirit of God:

Teach me the way of simplicity and surrender so that in this world of consumption, noise, and endless choices I might model joy, peace, and freedom.

Amen.

July 17
Longings for deeper divine union

Holy Spirit of God:

Lead me into the grace of healing.

Fill me with your peace as I feel the frictions of being human alongside the longings for deeper divine union.

Amen.

July 18
Blessing versus resistance

Divine Love Speaking to My Heart:

During this summer season, give me rhythms to rest and opportunities to soak in the experience of your love through silence, nature, and reading.

Quiet the chatter of my mental conversation and concerns with the peace of your presence.

Most of all, give me the quality of relating with others that bears forth the gift of blessing versus resistance, love versus judgment.

And for my travels, I ask the grace of safety and the gift of useful surprises and new friendships, especially when stressed by the demands of unfamiliar environments, unexpected delays, difficulties, and discomforts.

Amen.

July 19
Inspired by the encircled saints

Grace-Giver:

Inspired by the encircled saints, I re-dedicate my life to the movement of your love into this and every moment of my lifetime.

Amen.

July 20
The purpose of my arising in life

Beloved Mind of God, in Whom I Live and Move and Have My Being:

In union with Christ, lift me up into the life of Spirit, no longer controlled by impulses to resist growth or overindulge my appetites.

Now, I choose to use all life conditions as a path to observe the way I am, not just how others are or aren't.

Aware that the purpose of my arising in life is to mature in understanding, I take responsibility for my unfolding and request teachers of wisdom to show me the way to peace and truth.

Amen.

July 21
Your Word is made personal in the silence

Life Upon Life:

I come from you and return to you and in between learn how to love. You are with me, and beyond the veil of perception I am with you.

In this moment, your welcome is available in my return and your Word is made personal in the silence.

I remember, and grow quiet on the inside, aware that my true life is hidden with you.

Amen.

July 22

Make me beautiful on the inside

Jesus the Messiah:

You know me. I matter to you. You wish to make me beautiful on the inside, a simple reflection of your self-giving love.

I consent in silence to this interior renovation. Give me courage to observe my unloving words, gestures, and desires so I may become increasingly passive to the personality in me that wants to react, attack, or respond in the ways I have been taught by those who have forgotten love.

I belong to you. The beauty of love is my destination. Begin my second education into love by your Word and Spirit leading me deeper into your way, your truth, and your life.

Amen.

July 23
Feel what can't be proven

God Beyond All Comprehension:

Open me to the gift of light, waking me up inside to a life of love. You are ever-present right now underneath and beyond all things and thoughts.

I need look nowhere else than here, now, today declared and remembered: Christ in, with, and through me by the Spirit released from death and darkness, revealed in the vast gift of the present sweetly born in silence and surrender.

I won't try to understand. I give in and descend into my heart to feel what can't be proven.

Amen.

July 24
Wait in silence for the clarity of your counsel

God, my Counselor:

Imprint your love upon my heart.

Lead me to walk in your light.

Guide me in all I do and say so that my words may bear witness to your way.

With your Word in my heart, I delight more than in the riches of this world.

I wait in the silence for the clarity of your counsel.

Amen.

July 25
You who are the first light in the depths of the deep

God of Loving-kindness:

You who are the first light in the depths of the deep, shine unexpected blessings upon my life outstretched to you.

Draw me into your closeness and send me into the world with attentiveness to the movement of your kindness that can flow from you through me.

Amen.

July 26

The darkness of my fears

God My Healer:

Reach your hand into the darkness of my fears. Forgive my unholy ways. Let not the feeling of separation keep me from your heart.

Too long have I let fear control me, projecting onto others what I am unaware of within. May your perfect love cast every fear out from the chamber of my mind and memories.

Amen.

July 27

Walk in the future

You Who Birth the Future:

In your promises, I am inspired to walk in the future.

I am encouraged to listen for your voice calling to me even through the valleys of darkness and doubt.

Amen.

July 28
I am chased by your joy

God Who Brings Joy:

Touch my heartstrings and make your song come to life in me.

I am chased by your joy into new territory.

You have such a way with your extravagance.

What can I say? Phrases like "Here I am, Lord" and "Let it be in me, Lord" come to mind.

You turn my darkest howls into shouts of hosanna.

You have a way of making me your miracle.

I can see it with hindsight—always you were there, here, among the silence—infinite possibilities abounding.

Amen.

July 29
Your grace finds the seam in my heart

Holy Spirit of God:

Your grace finds the seam in my heart and follows it to the places waiting to be opened further by your love.

Lead me today by your gentle wisdom, guiding my way in commerce and culture.

In this silent surrender, I receive everything I need to face the next challenge.

May your grace work the seams in my heart, expanding my feeling of "I" to include the reality of you.

Amen.

July 30
Open hands into the morning light

God of This Moment:

I lift my open hands into the morning light to catch the present moment, this wise teacher revealing me to me.

I share my tears with the earth and remember the foundation upon which I live.

Your living Word rises up to meet me like the wind. Silently, suddenly you are here again in my heart awakening me for more love.

Your loving Word is all in all.

The summertime is for loving. I walk among the dewy grass and listen to the infinite moment.

I can see in this droplet just about to release and fall to the earth itself: Weeping Spirit. Crying love. Drenching light.

And it all helps me remember.

Amen.

July 31
I gently place my pain with you

God of Tender Love:

Broken by life and aware of my suffering, I gently place my pain with you.

May this prayer touch the merciful hearts of Jesus and his mother in just the right way that heals old wounds, nurturing present and future growth.

Amen.

AUGUST

It is as if God says to us:

My earth speaks to you in the stillness of summer mornings.

Press your ear upon the earth. Listen to my life.

You are a prayer happening forever in my heart.

You are my earth's keeper.

Your Brother Tree and Sister Sky wait for you to remember my family name pressed upon your own clay flesh made alive with my Spirit.

We are in this together.

Please, go deeper now into the listening, and remember.

August 1
Let peace become my companion

Beloved Comforter:

Let your love encircle and envelop me.

In your mercy raise me up.

Let peace become my companion.

Let me be reconciled with family and friends.

May I know you, O my loving companion presence.

Amen.

August 2
All things are possible

Christ My Healer:

Remind me that, with you, all things are possible. Help me not limit your power in my life today with any language of despair, restriction, or defeat.

Amen.

August 3
I cease my resistance

Beloved Trinity:

Thank you for the gift of life. Thank you for the rhythms of rest and work. Today, I request the vision to observe in myself what I so dislike in others.

Give me the grace of transformation so that I cease my resistance to love in the form of judgment and dislike of others.

Amen.

August 4
Move into the future

Deep Light of the Universe:

You call me to awaken to the gift of compassion.

Soften my heart to listen with care and to look with softness.

From the beginning, you have wished for me to be and keep inviting me to become.

Help me learn from the past and move into the future with the lessons of love.

Amen.

August 5
Change my tune to praise

Word Before the Beginning:

My words help shape my experience in life. Therefore, I wish to notice when I am complaining or critical. Change my tune to praise and gratitude.

Amen.

August 6
I reach out to receive your grace

Light of the World:

Dark emotions arising in reaction to difficulties in life reveal that my inner landscape is still in need of receiving your healing warmth.

Aware of my need for help, I reach out to receive your grace.

Amen.

August 7
Your love leads me

Silent Center:

In a world seeking the summit of success, you draw me into the small, quiet shadows of surrender.

There, you teach me the way of love through the humiliations of life.

In meekness you show me joy. In surrender you show me trust. In emptiness you provide for all my needs.

I thank you that your love leads me so that I don't have to lead myself to any summit other than the hill marked with a cross, revealing the true logic of self-giving in a world addicted to winning.

Amen.

August 8

Turning me more and more into love

Beloved Christ:

Awaken in me the awareness of my tone, gesture, and word choices.

I wish to more completely observe how I relate to others, and in observing gain understanding, and in understanding consent to your transforming life turning me more and more into love.

Amen.

August 9
God is the fullness of meaning

Sustainer of the Created:

May the light of God surround me.

May the life of God sustain me.

May the love of God enfold me.

May the power of God protect me.

May the presence of God nurture me.

May the promises of God inspire me.

I am not alone.

My life is not meaningless.

In the beginning was meaning.

God is the fullness of meaning and through your Word I partake in this meaningful life.

And all is well.

Amen.

August 10
The house of my soul awaits your indwelling

O My Life-giving God:

The house of my soul awaits your indwelling.

There are rooms that need renovation.

But Lord, how can this be when I dwell in you and you in me?

I wait for your arrival, only to discover you are already here with me.

Amen.

August 11
Expand my capacity to bear and share love

Loving and Holy God:

Expand my capacity to bear and share love. I know that something in me must become more like a child if I am to enter your kingdom. May this process begin with the lessening of my vanity and pride.

Amen.

August 12
Increase my desire to delight in you

Beloved Trinity:

Increase my desire to delight in you.

Cleanse my will so that I desire what delights you.

Fill my mind with impressions that inspire wonder so that I live in correspondence with your heart of love, radiating the beauty and joy of your intentions.

Amen.

August 13
A graceful alchemy

O Lord:

If it happens that during this day I feel myself pressed into a particular emotion or thought, I call upon you now to remind me then that whatever it is that I am feeling is not me.

Convey to me now in the silent space of this prayer the feeling of strength to carry me through moments of weakness.

Now, in this still moment, I request for my life a graceful alchemy of water into wine, and wine into life, and life into love, and love into the light of Christ, and Christ into all in all.

Amen.

August 14
Holding me together in love as I grow

Abba:

Thank you for holding me together in love as I grow. Open my heart to receive your living Word deeply. Sustain me in my life efforts so I may be refreshed by your Spirit in worship and rest.

Amen.

August 15

I wish to live the mystery of Christ

Living and Loving God:

I wish to live the mystery of Christ, not just know or speak about it.

I wish for your Spirit to take hold of my life and liberate me from my fears, anxieties, demands, and desires.

I wish to make Christ alive in me through relationships, respect, and self-giving.

Lord, I wish to no longer be the person I have always been, but to become the person you have destined me to be in Christ.

Amen.

August 16
The one necessary thing

Most Loving God:

Awake now to the gift of life, I wish to do the one necessary thing—to turn to you and your influences. Amidst all the alternatives, I choose you.

Your grace and love are awakening me, turning me, softening me. I respond like a sunflower in sync with the light. You are my life. You are my love.

Amen.

August 17
Unmask my fears and worries

Gracious and Merciful Heavenly Father:

Pour out your Spirit upon me that I might feel your presence in the opening movements of this day. As I am drawn into the holiness of love and the strength of community, unmask my fears and worries as useless.

I choose the gift of your love, and in this love, I flourish.

Amen.

August 18
Open to your love

Song of My Deepest Faith:

Open to your love, I feel you teaching me through the simple movements of my day. Certain that you are with me, I trust that all things today will work together for my good.

Amen.

August 19

Returning to you in surrender

Beloved One:

Bless all students returning to school.

Bless all teachers returning to teach.

Bless all leaders returning to lead.

Bless all workers returning to labor.

Bless all beggars returning for more.

Bless all hearts returning to you in surrender.

Remind me that your gift of grace takes me all the way.

Amen.

August 20
I feel your loving presence

Most Loving and Holy Trinity:

I wish to feel the fire of your presence radiating through me, melting away shortcomings of personality that deplete my force for love and joy. Do unto me what I cannot do for myself: heal, transform, and overcome.

Such gifts are enough, Lord. I feel your loving presence and surrender my ways to your way.

Amen.

August 21
The name of Jesus fills the empty spaces

Beloved:

Nourish me in your springs of silence in the inner room of my heart, where the name of Jesus fills the empty spaces with grace, and where my consent to him leads me deeper into your love.

Amen.

August 22

Under the shadow of grace

Abba:

Under the shadow of grace, I pray to discover more of the unfolding largeness of your love.

Where can I go where you are not with me?

Who can I be where you will not meet me?

Show me my fears, that I may not be driven by them. Show me where my heart closes to love, that I may learn to open to it in the presence of fear and worry.

Taught in the silence of the heart, I learn the nature of listening for your Word so to be a vessel of grace.

Amen.

August 23

The strong circle of your way, truth, and life

Beloved Strength of Life:

I wish to live today in the strong circle of your way, truth, and life.

Help me see myself more clearly today—the negative and the positive. I do not want to live in the darkness of denial. I want to live in the light of insight.

Amen.

August 24

I call to mind the beauty of wilderness

Abba:

Embraced in the personal care that I feel in places of beauty, I feel more aware that nothing can separate me from your love in Christ. I call to mind the beauty of wilderness and hold that view in my heart as an icon of your living presence.

Silence. Solitude. Expansive spaces of graceful trees—such places portend the essence of the soul, where you invite me into deeper love and life.

Amen.

August 25
The silence of your heart

Abba:

Awaken me to the feeling of "I" hidden in you.

The beginning of all things is in the silence of your heart, and I can rest there always, including right now.

Amen.

August 26
Under the shelter of your name

Abiding Presence:

Remind me that under the shelter of the name of Jesus Christ, all is victorious. All threads of lies and darkness are pulled back to their ends and frayed open in this name's light and love. These knots and threads no longer hold me.

Today, I wish to live under the shelter of your name and in the knowledge that names are like beams of light proceeding in front of me, revealing the nature of the one referred.

And your name is the eternal Word, which was in the beginning, is now, and will always be. Within the shelter of this name, I live, and move, and have my being.

Amen.

August 27
Your Word shapes me

Deep, Living Water:

I wish to drink from your springs of silence and feel the difference your presence makes in the quiet stillness.

I shape this silence into prayer as your Word shapes me into a servant.

Amen.

August 28
Created for union with you

Christ My Love, Wisdom, and Beauty:

Help me remember that my needs for survival, power, and love do not solely define me. I am also created for union with you.

Awaken me with your Word. Increase my hunger and thirst for your presence in the silence.

Amen.

August 29
Help me listen

Living Gate into Abundant Life:

Where in me am I blind to your truth?

Where in my life am I deaf to the calling of your living Word spoken in the silence?

Aware of my limitations, help me listen.

Then, birth wisdom, love, and truth through me.

Amen.

August 30
With the dawn I rise

Holy Love, Holy God:

With the dawn I rise by the gift of your light in the face of Christ, whose love claims me this moment and lifts me up from the confusion of life into the truth of who I am and where I come from.

In the hours of this day, regardless of what I am doing or where I am going, I ask for increasing purity of heart and attention to your Spirit, my inner companion of high truth and eternal love.

Amen.

August 31
Opening my heart to surrender

Eternal Listener:

I rejoice that you touch my life with a strong grace, opening my heart to surrender. It is impossible to explain. Awaiting my return, again and again your presence is asking me, “Will you love me now?”

Yes, in this moment, I say yes to you, my source.

Amen.

SEPTEMBER

It is as if God says to us:

Return to me and let me instruct you.

Learn my wisdom that leads to freedom and my freedom that leads to love.

September 1
Activate in my mind

Spirit of God:

Awaken me into the fullness of your knowing and lead me into the depths of your truth. Activate in my mind the capacity to understand Scripture and share love-inspired insights with others.

Amen.

September 2
Release me from past shames and present fears

Almighty God, My Source and Sustainer:

Guide me on the threefold journey of purification, illumination, and union with you.

Tame my passions that inhibit my flourishing and keep me asleep to the mind of your Spirit.

Release me from past shames and present fears.

Amen.

September 3
The center of your love

Lord Jesus, Living Christ:

In the silence, speak your Word. Transform my insecurities into empathy and my needs into miracles.

In every situation that seems overwhelming to me today, let silence lead me to the center of your love and the embrace of your truth.

Amen.

September 4
Take me deeper

Eternal Love and Source of Life:

Take me deeper into Scripture to personally experience the awareness of your nearness beyond the printed page.

I wish to enter the mystery of faith touched by your Spirit and infused with your love.

Amen.

September 5
The fruit of your love

Womb of Life:

Bear in me the fruit of your love. Show me the way to love those I may dislike. Walk with me into every friction as I welcome your life in me with faith.

Amen.

September 6
The mirage of my falseness

Living Forgiveness, Everlasting Grace:

Humbled by my unconscious and unloving behavior, I give thanks for the way in which life can become my teacher. I ask for the courage to see clearly through the mirage of my falseness into the truth of who I am in you, Lord Jesus Christ.

Amen.

September 7
Provision upon my life today

Most Gracious and Loving Heavenly Father:

Pour provision upon my life today.

Ground me in the life-giving presence of your living Word and deepen my understanding of the way of loving service.

Amen.

September 8
You have created my soul and given to me a secret strength

Most Glorious and Perfect Source of Love:

You have created my soul and given to me a secret strength in my visible body. I am flesh and spirit. Because of this, I am a hybrid, adapted for two worlds—this one of forms and feelings and your world.

You are my most perfect source of love.

Amen.

September 9
The everlasting hiddenness of your love

Beloved:

I retreat deeper into your silence. There, beyond all books and beliefs, I simply feel your loving presence.

"How can this be?" I ask.

And it is as if your Spirit speaks: "Because of me. It is me. It is all me."

My God, my God, you have not forsaken me! All along it has been you—higher and deeper than thought, the everlasting hiddenness of your love revealed in Christ in whom my life is now found.

Amen.

September 10
You are always with me

Loving God of the Universe:

Your journey to me has set me on a journey to you. While it is tempting to think that I am all alone on this journey, in Christ I discover that you are always with me, and that I am also with brothers and sisters in our silence and in our speaking.

Help me become a vibrant participant in this spiritual community today.

Help me to see in others something of myself and in so doing feel our common humanity and your uncommon grace, in the realm of this beating heart and the field of life that is the human family.

Amen.

September 11
In the silence I feel your love

Comfort of the Suffering:

In the remembrance of moments seared with shock, I pray to connect more deeply with the meaning of life. I wish for personal knowledge and direct experience with your deepest purpose and meaning.

Hidden in the heart of this human experience is silence, and in the silence I feel your love. In the silence I discover your presence, and in your presence I find purpose.

I join my prayer today in the silence, requesting help on the journey into forgiveness and surrender.

Amen.

September 12
Feed me with your living stillness

Beloved of My Heart:

You have called me to listen. Draw me into the heart of prayer. Feed me with your living stillness. Calm me with your vast love.

I request this very personal experience today.

I gain strength through stillness, resting in the warmth of your name. Speak to my heart by the mystery of your Spirit, Word, and sacrament, reminding me as I go about my daily activities that you are the beloved of my heart.

Amen.

September 13
Resting in you, I remember

Eternal Light of Attention:

Resting in you, I remember myself, and in so doing, I remember you. In this busy world, it is easy to forget.

Today, I wish to rise in remembrance, receiving knowledge and wisdom in my heart. Although there appear to be many paths for my life, I feel drawn to this path of quietness in gentleness and surrender.

In my solitary silence you kiss my soul, and I feel more alive.

Amen.

September 14
Born in the mystery of your love

Joyful Song Beyond My Soul:

Born in the mystery of your love, I begin this day surrendering all my confusions and questions to your explanatory power. I request personal attention for such situations that seem bewildering to my natural mind, trusting your help will arrive.

Amen.

September 15
I am sustained by your power

Beloved Life-giver:

I am grateful for the gift of life that is occurring in me at this moment, conveyed to me a millisecond at a time. I stand in awe that I am sustained by your power.

I recognize I am not controlling this thing called "being alive." It is a constant gift flowing to me, set in motion by your grace.

I wish to use this gift of life to nourish my being and the well-being of others through the accumulation of love and wisdom.

Amen.

September 16

Speak to my heart in the secret chamber of the Spirit

Abba:

Speak to my heart in the secret chamber of the Spirit where I feel love and know the taste of beauty and goodness. I shall listen and wait.

My day-to-day living is full of many concerns and tasks. But you have left me a trail of living Words to lead me to yourself. Such Words are felt more than known.

Explanation spoils the lion's leap. And I feel your presence in silence and beauty and wisdom and love.

I stand in awe of what this means—your speaking and leaping. I won't ever figure it out, but I can feel it like music. And so, I listen and wait until it is my turn to be like a resonant cello calling forth from its inner chamber vibrations of love and beauty.

Amen.

September 17
The blessing of assured understanding

Most Loving and Almighty God:

The world and my life situation are often cluttered with confusing choices. As I face decisions and make requests for guidance today, I ask for the blessing of assured understanding that you alone can give.

Amen.

September 18
The ever-deepening experience of consciously chosen love

Beloved All in All:

I wish to feel gratitude for every person with whom I interact. I call them to mind with the eyes of my heart. I remember the ways in which I felt provoked, unaccepted, or judged, and I wish to see where I provoked, rejected, and judged others.

Help me release these feelings and actions into your forever sky of forgiveness, which is free and available when I look up from my toil.

Where I have felt wronged, help me forgive.

Where I have felt blessed, help me give thanks.

In all things I request the ever-deepening experience of consciously chosen love over against negative reactions.

Amen.

September 19
Nurtured into the presence of your life

Beautiful Savior:

Graced by the beauty of creation, I am nurtured into the presence of your life. Thank you for moments of wonder lost in the silence of your embrace. In the temple of my heart, I resist the temptation to just think about it.

I wish to also feel it and experience the warming gift of your life-giving love in and through every moment—all gentle invitations to surrender my striving and trust your providing.

Amen.

September 20

The truth of my being one with others in you

Ever-living God of Peace:

Aware of the transforming power of united thoughts and feelings on a global scale, I stand in awe of my participation in and as the living, breathing body of Christ.

Help me experience with direct awareness the truth of my being one with others in you.

Forgive me for forgetting through regressing to fear and division. I am yours, and beyond all self-generated words or pictures, you are the living source of life and love.

Amen.

September 21
The shadow of your light

Beloved Silence:

Thank you for listening to my confessions and failures. Under the shadow of your light, my darkness is no more.

Amen.

September 22
Reaching for something more

Lord God of All Creation:

I confess that culture cannot satisfy the longing of my heart. I am reaching for something more today and stretch forth into your grace through these prayer words.

You are the direction my life desires.

You are the love my being requires.

You are the light to which my soul aspires, and I praise you for meeting me with grace.

Amen.

September 23

Help me rest in you

Most Loving and Gracious God:

Swayed by the speed of life, my soul feels dizzy and disoriented. Your rest beckons. The silence of your presence rises in my heart, and I wish to take rest here.

Drawn by the gravity of your presence, I am held strong through the cycles of life. Help me rest in you, even while I also move and have my being amidst busy comings, goings, and doings.

Amen.

September 24
Open to love in this world of pain

Loving God:

Help me stay open to love in this world of pain. In my hurt, I often close down. Open me with the gift of forgiveness.

In my worry, I often turn inward. Lift my gaze to your future.

In my loneliness, I often feel unworthy. Remind me of my infinite value as a participant in your divine nature.

In all things, draw me to your presence, available now in the interior realms of silence and surrender.

Amen.

September 25
Awake now to the presence of your love

Beloved Lord Jesus Christ:

Awake now to the presence of your love, I feel you holding my life. I wish to see your strength reaching into the depths of my suffering. You are providing a way out, a way out that comes from above.

I wish to receive this gift and be lifted further into the light of your wisdom and experience the attraction to your truth and love radiating from your Word.

Amen.

September 26
The delight of your living presence

Joy of My Heart, Laughter of My Soul:

Help me feel the delight of your living presence in the midst of any moments of despair. By your Spirit, fill me with a lighthearted gratefulness for the gift of life, reflecting joy in my words, gestures, and countenance.

Amen.

September 27

Seal now the truths I gain in the silence this day

Beloved Presence:

Seal now the truths I gain in the silence this day by the power of your Spirit so that I may rise into the person you are calling me to become. You are my God and I belong to you. Make me fully alive in you.

Amen.

September 28

Drawing me closer to the center of your loving heart

Beloved Center:

I am grateful for the opportunity to remember and receive your grace. I wish to rest in you, my center, as I move about the circumference of my daily duties.

In the gentle silence of prayerful moments, reveal more completely the meaning of my life, drawing me closer to the center of your loving heart, healing the self that is scattered by this life's situations, suffering, and sadness.

Amen.

September 29

Let the incarnation continue

Beloved Lord Jesus Christ:

You are the living truth that shapes the contours of my life.

You are the love that brings life to bear in my barrenness.

You are the open ground from which the way is revealed.

Today, I wish to experience your truth, life, and way in direct astonishment of things revealed. In labor with angels bearing me up, I pray: let this transformation come quickly.

To the praise of your inner work in me, let the incarnation continue through me today.

Amen.

September 30
Say yes to wise choices

Holy Trinity:

For you, O God, I wish to live, surrendered to your living Word, helping me to say yes to wise choices with integrity, harmony, and joy.

Amen.

OCTOBER

It is as if God says to us:

Earnestly receive the colored light of this new day as my strength.

There is something to be gained in you through the silence of this pearled morning.

Listen. Wait. It is deeper than your thoughts. Feel it through your body.

Fearlessly open to my love!

Be encouraged, not afraid, by the powers that be and always remember:

Nurture your relationship with me, your Source. Don't worry about the sideshows. All is well. Every relationship is my temple. I celebrate its quality, not its kind. Love is the quality of my heart, wooing you into a bigger life than you can imagine or control. Enjoy this journey, beloved ones!

Laugh from your belly. It may help loosen love and get it flowing, especially with your adversaries.

October 1

Hold me close to your heart of love

Most Loving and Gracious God:

In my moments and hours of confusion, bring your clarity.

In my episodes of pain, bring your comfort.

In my awareness of being out of sorts, bring your peace.

I am unfolding. As I do, hold me close to your heart of love, giving me the assurance of things unseen. When day and night bring difficulties, sustain me.

Amen.

October 2

An elegant movement in the dance of becoming

Yes, Abba:

I wish to move in the circle of your truth, under the influence of your love and with the sway of your grace.

Make me an elegant movement in the dance of becoming that is the gift of your life in Christ.

Your faithfulness is cast wide in the firmament above and beneath all things. I feel its strength speaking. In this face of grace that is Christ, there is nothing that separates me from your love.

In this open circumference, help me live and move and have my being—beyond everything else I am asked, compelled, and tempted to do or be today.

Amen.

October 3
To feel the beauty of October

Beloved Creator of the Heavens and the Earth:

I wish to feel and experience a deeper union with you. I set aside the hours of this day to feel the beauty of October and know that this season visibly demonstrates my journey back to you.

May I be born, flourish, and release back into your breath.

Amen.

October 4
Clues to the meaning of my life

Loving God:

Aware of your faithfulness to humankind, I surrender to your living Word and wisdom that are coming to me at just the right time.

I thank you for these clues to the meaning of my life and my purpose.

Stronger together with you than apart, I wish to delight in you this day and know in this community of prayer that nothing can separate me from your love in Christ.

Amen.

October 5
The wonder of your rest

Holy Spirit:

Open the center and guide me into the wonder of your rest.

Whatever occurs in my external life today, I wish to remember that my inner life is hidden in God through Christ always.

Amen.

October 6
I am rising this morning to receive

Eternal Love:

Your truth lights the day and your way unfolds into love.

Whatever dreams and difficulties the dark hours delivered, I am rising this morning to receive your eternal love.

Words can't capture its velocity.

Images can't contain its mass.

Your love is infinite, immediately present under, beyond, in, and through every sense, thought, and feeling I have about myself or another.

Like the sunrise, you change everything. I lift my heart in praise.

Amen.

October 7
Anoint me with awareness

Holy Spirit of God:

Pour down upon me the rain of your life, light, and love.

Anoint me with awareness.

I wait for your movements drawing me deeper into the silence of your love, making all things new.

Amen.

October 8
The wind-words bring stillness

Holy God of My Deepening Journey:

My prayer words are meant to be like wind in tall prairie grass. The Spirit blows where it will.

Within, there are many grasses, wheat, tares, weeds—all mixed together. Gentle are you who tend my heart, knowing one from the other.

But in the open expanse of being, your words come like wind and stir the grasses, moving like waves: some smooth and stretched out, others crashing and erratic.

There is a way to stand still in the center of the vastness. Though the grass is over my head, I can feel your living words moving in my heart.

The wind-words bring stillness. Feeling is beyond listening. And your Spirit is beyond the feeling. Sheer prairie presence.

Amen.

October 9

The sum of divine oneness

Most Merciful and Loving God:

I accept the fact that I can't fix myself. So I welcome again the gift of contemplative prayer, wherein I participate in the interior experience of moving beyond faith into the sphere of your Spirit's work, multiplying even the smallest ounce of faith into the sum of divine oneness.

Amen.

October 10

Your presence is an expanding center

Holy Love, Unending Life, Invincible Light:

I wish to enter your house of being and sit at your banquet of wisdom. Your invitation is calling, and time is a factor. While I spend much of my life and energy doing, I wish to also be with you. Light my way into the inner room of my heart. Your presence is an expanding center, day by day dissolving more of myself and revealing more of Christ. May I decrease, and may you increase.

In your house of being there is only one law: the law of love. Forsaken by life, I turn to your love and there find abundant life in union with Christ, who has pledged never to leave or forsake me.

I need to go no farther than my breath and beating heart. I hear you now; it's as if you are saying to my soul: Sit. Be still and understand that I am with you as holy love, unending life, invincible light.

Amen.

October 11

Strength to resist all temptations

Beloved Jesus, Lord of Light:

I wish to feel your life-giving presence through the gifts of silence, sermon, sacrament, and Scripture. May the beauty revealed in the undoing of summer by the forces of fall instruct me on my own spiritual journey. May this day establish me deeper in the vibrant soil of your resurrection power, offering to me strength to resist all temptations to despair of any approaching darkness.

Amen.

October 12

Hope to hear your words of promise

Loving God:

For any difficulties I may face today, I request wisdom to see the situation from a new perspective.

For any fear I may feel today, I request peace to touch the provocation with neutralizing faith.

For any depression I may taste today, I request hope to hear your words of promise in the deep places of my being.

Amen.

October 13
Bring about the best possible future

Lord God of All Creation:

Anoint me with your Holy Spirit and let the mind of Christ become available to me. Open me to the unlimited possibilities of good you have in store for me.

Feed me with your Spirit of wisdom, love, and understanding for each situation and person I encounter, and bring about the best possible future for my transformation in Christ.

Amen.

October 14

Onward in prayer through all the seasons

Lord of the Seasons:

I await the revealing of barren branches and windy November nights. I feel life changing around me. I feel it in my body. Like the earth, I too am in transition: a pilgrim on my way to your heart.

I encounter sickness and am humbled; yet healing is provided.

I walk through depression and feel overwhelmed; yet new thinking emerges.

Beyond this earth there is still more of you and your creation.

Beyond all my troubles and disappointments, you are, and all is well.

Lifted into the silent mystery of my heart unveiled to your unyielding love, I journey onward in prayer through all the seasons of this life's earthly passage.

Amen.

October 15
Uphold me in every endeavor

Abba:

Pour out your Spirit upon my seeking mind and illuminate my path with your wisdom. Seal into my cells the radiance of your love and uphold me in every endeavor, so that I might become the fullest expression of your abundant intention for human life. Your name is "I Am," so that I might be.

I celebrate the gift of life given each moment in and through the living presence of Christ, your Son, who will never leave me or forsake me. Whatever day it is, your Word says it is the same yesterday, today, and tomorrow.

In you I live and move and have my being.

Amen.

October 16
The pull of your grace

Divine Love Who Draws Me Close:

Silently draw me close by the pull of your grace, lifting me out of the gravity field of myself.

Amen.

October 17
Bring a new and different kind of life

Light of the World:

Whatever darkness I may find in my life today, I pray to be awakened by your rays of love. Give me soft eyes to see the particles of praise shimmering in the sunlight of consciously chosen love. I wish to stay open-hearted even when I see the chaos of human behavior. Help me trust that your light will illuminate my inner realms to bring a new and different kind of life.

Amen.

October 18
Joy despite the sorrow

Lord Jesus Christ:

Let me feel your living presence as strength beneath the silence, love beyond the fear, and joy despite the sorrow.

Feed me this day with your wisdom. Cultivate in me the seed of your love that leads to deeper community. Remove in me any obstacles to love and truth.

Amen.

October 19
Awaken to my possible evolution in Christ

God of Heaven and Earth:

The wordless wonder of your creation invites me to look up. When my own heart closes to love, remind me of the heavenly streams of creation above. Help me awaken to my possible evolution in Christ, walking with your Word and your wisdom and all those who have gone before me.

Amen.

October 20

Clothe me in the raiment of your wisdom

God of This and Every Moment:

Clothe me in the raiment of your wisdom.

I rejoice in my freedom from whatever situation may be occurring in life.

In perfect trust, I simply give thanks for this day with joy.

Amen.

October 21

The certitude of presence available

Lord Jesus, Living Christ:

Thank you for the certitude of presence available in the Eucharist.

Thank you for the communion of saints who journey with me.

Thank you for the gift of being an embodied spiritual being capable of giving, receiving, and becoming love.

Amen.

October 22

Grounded, I can ascend

Jesus Christ, My Life:

You are teaching me that you are silent, living, and radiant. You are revealing to me that you are life from life and God from God.

Your eternal Word is the nameless name above all other names. You are helping me recognize that in you I live and move and have my being, and that this truth is the beginning of my most enduring freedom. Grounded, I can ascend.

Amen.

October 23

My source of loving community

Loving Trinity:

Help me to meet the people and events of this day with an open heart. I wish to become love. No matter how I may be received, I thank you for being my source of loving community.

Amen.

October 24
A temple of love

Abba:

Resting in your silence, I begin to see and feel that my heart is a sanctuary of your everlasting Spirit—a shelter for the highest, a temple of love.

I begin to participate in the sphere of wisdom, opening me to further depths of your truth.

I am a humble body yet imbued with the music of your grace.

Christ is my hymn sung through this particular chord of embodiment. The tune resonates in the central chambers, a cadence leading me back home to you with every beat.

Amen.

October 25
A vessel of your reflected glory

Living Christ:

I pray to rise with the sun and feel your radiance in my heart. Downcast no longer, I rise with joy, love, and peace. You are giving to me the gift of consciousness, and I wish to live as a vessel of your reflected glory. Light from light, I worship you, the light of the world.

Amen.

October 26
Draw me deeper

Abba:

Saturate my heart with the outstanding qualities of your Spirit. Draw me deeper into your presence beyond the silence. I ask for help today for all the questions I ponder and live with. Where I object to the way things are, help me to live in trust.

Help me to hold my interpretations of reality loosely, gently, and humbly, in the recognition that you can transform my apparatus of perception to experience all things differently in the light of your love.

Amen.

October 27

An unfailing guide

Beloved of My Deepest Self:

Help me to remember today that you are an unfailing guide, showing me the way through all of life's events into the peace that passes all understanding.

Amen.

October 28

Life is an eternal gift

Heart of God:

Help me to see that each moment of life is an eternal gift packed with possibilities.

I recognize and declare that in Christ nothing can separate me from your love, and therefore I am indeed not far from your presence.

Amen.

October 29
Mold the darkness of my mind

God of Now and Then, Here and There:

I wait in silence for truth to shape itself in me. Mold the darkness of my mind with the light of your wisdom, fired in the kiln of eternity until golden hot and flowing forth from the Word, love making me and all things very good.

You are forming Christ in me through this journey into love, goodness, and wisdom.

Thank you for this purpose that gives holy meaning to my lifetime.

Amen.

October 30

You are Mary's Mystery and Joseph's Dream

Lord Jesus, Living Christ:

You are the friend of women and children and the refuge of all forsaken by life.

You are the servant of servants. You are the first and last.

You are a little child, yet also the eternal Word in whom all things dwell.

You are Mary's mystery and Joseph's dream.

You are my all in all.

You are midwife to all souls and tender mother to all broken hearts.

You are the suffering one who understands our human loneliness, brokenness, and betrayals.

You are time and no-time. You are space and beyond space.

You are. You have been. You shall be.

You are this and so much more, and in you I live.

Amen.

October 31
Connect my life with your love

God of Immense Love:

Connect my life with your love more completely, so that in the upheavals of life I feel sustained by the strength of silence.

Reveal to me the capacity of how I can further participate in what your love is doing in this incomprehensible world that meets me with joy and suffering, peace and conflict.

Through my life journeys, awaken me to become love.

Amen.

NOVEMBER

It is as if God is saying to us:

Trust me.

I'm with you through your family gatherings and holiday travels.

This is a quiet time for the earth.

Listen to the soft snow starting.

Let the cold draw you deeper into the warmth of my love.

I'm right here.

November 1
Brief is this way of being

Lord God of All Creation:

Every day I circle the sun on this sacred, living sphere. You have choreographed these moves, keeping good rhythm. During these longer nights and shorter days of November, kindle in my heart the light of Christ. Let this light be manifest in the form of love, wisdom, and directed living toward your blazing glory.

Thank you for the awareness of the cycles of time and the recognition that time is a factor. Brief is this way of being; your eternity is calling. Therefore, I light my candles early, sleep, and surrender more and more to the light of your love in Christ.

Amen.

November 2
Turn my words into song

Beloved Spirit of God:

Anoint me with the silence of your strength. However this day may unfold, stabilize my heart with the ballast of Scripture.

Turn my reading into listening.

Turn my words into song.

Turn my being into becoming, lest I cease to grow.

Amen.

November 3
The grace of giving

Loving God:

Where I feel tangled up in wanting and constricted in love, gently open me to the grace of giving and the freedom of fellowship. When I take others negatively, help me release this way of being and receive your grace.

Amen.

November 4
How could I ever feel alone

Beloved God:

Remind me that your life is living me. Your love is holding me.

Your presence is surrounding me. Your being is blessing me.

Your wisdom is guiding me. Your light is leading me.

Your creation is nurturing me. Your power is protecting me.

Your will is shaping me. Your name is claiming me.

Your Son is healing me. Your Spirit is transforming me.

How could I ever feel alone?

Amen.

November 5
Infuse my life with wisdom

Christ of the Ages:

Teach me to live in your joy, fearless of all that could be and courageous in all that is. May the vertical power of your love infuse my life with wisdom beyond the horizontal powers of this external world.

Amen.

November 6
Rise in faith

Heavenly Father, Sustainer of This and Every Moment:

Touch my mind with the reverence that is the beginning of all spiritual wisdom and the yeast that makes me rise in faith.

Amen.

November 7

On this personal journey into your love

Lord Jesus Christ:

You truly contain within yourself the love I long for. Your compassion meets me in unexpected silent moments and sustains me in every dimension of my day.

Where I find unfairness, bring me inner balance.

On this personal journey into your love, I am set free from the demands of others' expectations and invited into the joy of simply being with you.

Amen.

November 8
Chance is random, but your grace is certain

God of Certitude:

I wish to live under the power of your will and hold in prayer those beloved to me, near and far. Knowing that chance is random, but your grace is certain, I place myself and those I love into the certitude of your loving care.

Amen.

November 9
A lamp of spiritual wisdom

God of Light:

I wish to acquire within my mind a lamp of spiritual wisdom so I will not stumble in the darkness I may confront today. Guide my steps by your Son and infuse me with the illumination Christ conveys in the Gospels, the Eucharist, and the cosmos.

Amen.

November 10
I am supported

God of Truth:

I request wisdom to grow in compassion toward others. In this sustaining relationship, one for the other, help me to see how I am supported by unknown brothers and sisters, especially:

Those who grow food and supply clean water.

Those who defend and decide.

Those who drive long distances to bring milk from farms and grapes from faraway vineyards.

Awake to the deep interconnectivity of our human system, I am humbled to play my role in the name of your love.

Amen.

November 11

In the circle of my friends and family

God of Life:

I pray to feel wholeness today in the circle of my friends and family. Where there are tensions, bring your peace. Where there is sickness, bring your healing. Where there is confusion, bring your clarity. As I stand in your love, bring me your joy.

Amen.

November 12

Your sustaining web of life

God of Peace:

I wish to stand fearless in the web of your presence, assured in every season and situation that you walk with me. In every realm of reality, I am upheld by your sustaining web of life, which nurtures me into the fullness of who I am destined to be.

Amen.

November 13
Help me to love

God of Insight:

I request wisdom to live in this world of relationships. Help me as problems rise and fall in my day. Lord Jesus, help me to love my neighbor as I love myself and to experience your way of being. You are with me always.

Amen.

November 14
A force for love

God of the Silence:

Calm and quiet my soul at the fount of your loving presence.

In your silence, replenish me with a force for love, especially for those who are the most demanding. When there is nowhere else to go, inspire me to drop into my heart and find your life-giving grace there, weaving the fabric of human reality into a tapestry of love.

Amen.

November 15
Hear the call of your love

God of Space and Time:

Give me a listening heart to hear the call of your love. Infinite and vast, beyond all time and space, yet also right here and now, you show me the beauty of your presence. Thank you for this day and all the experiences it will offer.

Amen.

November 16
Our extraordinary ordinariness

Almighty and Loving God:

I thank you for the gift of life. For the sake of the human community, I request that we might become the fullness of what you intend for us to be, right where we are in all our extraordinary ordinariness.

Amen.

November 17

Awake to the reality

Abba:

I am awake to the reality of your emerging and eternal life happening right now in the depth of my being. I feel connected to all people and to you, in whom I live and move and have my being. My present and eternal existence is assured through this union.

Amen.

November 18
More alive today than ever

Divine Teacher:

Grateful for the gift of life, I wish to feel more alive today than ever before.

Grateful for the experience of love, I wish to share more compassion.

I am aware that these gifts are to be recognized, received, and shared.

Where I think these gifts have not been given, I request courage to act as if they have, and in so acting become what I think I lack.

Amen.

November 19
Let me become the way toward transformation

Living Christ:

I am drawn to you as your Word and grace open my heart.

I request to be fed by your love and truth. I ask to feast with you in the silence.

Where there is stress, let me be the peace.

Where there is anger, let me be the forgiveness.

Where there are patterns of pain, let me become the way toward transformation.

Drawn to you, I surrender to the graceful possibilities you enable. For this I truly give thanks.

Amen.

November 20
The dark night infused with your light

God of Color, Warmth, and Light:

The northern nights are nearing, turning forest and field into scenes of passion.

The colored palettes of oaks and maples have sung their autumnal lullaby to summer, in tune with earthen hues of prairie grass.

It is time to gather into silence for a future season of growth.

I remember these ancient rhythms of sun and earth tilting in tandem.

I turn my heart toward your eternal home and warmth, ready for the dark night infused with your light.

Amen.

November 21
The solace of your company

Holy Spirit of God:

Turning now toward the solace of your company, I feel your presence and give thanks.

Be to my heart its deepest desire.

Be to my mind its fullest expression.

Be to my will its truest aim.

Amen.

November 22
Embraced in the center of your encompassing truth

Living One Whose Love Pulses Through the Creation:

Embraced in the center of your encompassing truth, I discover that in you there is no circumference. You can take it all. You embrace all dimensions of myself and awaken me further into your way, your truth, and your life.

In Christ, show me how your love pours into this sphere of life, intersecting as a cross, embracing my humanity—all of it.

Amen.

November 23

Your eternal love weaves into the history of things

I offer no resistance to you, O Lord my God, for from your creative power flash forth the particles of light that form into stars and galaxies.

I offer no resistance to you, O Lord my God, for your eternal love weaves into the history of things a kindness for the human species formed in your image.

For every delight I experience as a member of the human community, I give thanks.

For every suffering I seek to avoid yet encounter, I give thanks.

All of life is a gift.

With tenderness, with joy, and with laughter, I give thanks.

Amen.

November 24
Enter days of feasting

O Lord God With and Through Us:

As I enter days of feasting, help me create space for your presence.

As I partake in days of travel, help me take time for rest.

As I reunite with family, help me see in myself the thing I secretly or blatantly resist and by which I judge them.

Help me become love in the ordinary gathering of people, friends, neighbors, and family.

Amen.

November 25
My heart in service

God of my Gratitude:

In thanksgiving and praise I find a clue to the meaning of my life; a crumb from the bread of everything. I taste and see Christ's Mother's tears shed under the star of Bethlehem and in the shadow of the cross. What mystery did she know of this secret indwelling of the highest?

What might I too discover in the silence of all the ages past now lifted to my lips in the cup of Christ's presence?

As I am fed by love, help me lift my heart in service to the hungry and forsaken too.

Amen.

November 26
Hold me together

Living Life and Sustaining Love:

Help me feel in the universe your attracting grace, which keeps everything from coming apart.

May the Word of Christ hold me together with wisdom and love.

I give thanks for your Word and consent to being held by it so to remain at peace with you.

Amen.

November 27
Your center expands to my circumference

Beloved Companion of My Heart:

Your center expands to my circumference and I feel alive again.

Your life keeps me connected beyond my immediate concerns to love and serve you and others.

From the gift of your recharging love, I am filled to share, and for this I truly give thanks.

Amen.

November 28
My full attention

Most Gracious God of Love:

You have journeyed with me through this year of Sundays—Epiphany, Easter, Ascension, Pentecost, and the long stretch of ordinary green growth. Now I approach the candles of Advent.

I wish to give you my full attention so I may experience your fullness of life. As I enter through the gates of thanksgiving into the kingdom of Advent, reign in love on the throne of my heart, anointing me with the name Emmanuel.

Amen.

November 29

The presence of care

Holy God, Name Beyond All Names:

Your love announces to my innermost fears and insecurities an intention to transform me into a vessel of your life.

With Mary I surrender to the presence of care raising me to meet any unexpected events as a bearer of Christ.

Through this silent formation you touch my life so deeply that a new name appears upon the mantel of my heart, manifesting security and fearlessness beyond my capacity to create.

I praise you for naming me as a child of the highest.

Amen.

November 30
To live amidst the shadows of the past

Light of the World:

Open my heart and open my mind to your goodness and love.

Show me the way to live amidst the shadows of the past in the light of your forgiveness.

Amen.

DECEMBER

It is as if God is saying to us:

You now enter the deepest days of darkness.

Take time to recall through story and song the message of my descent to you in love.

While it's an ancient story told with the poetry of a different era, remember this: I surprise with wonder. I make the impossible, glorious.

Watch. Wait. Wonder.

December 1
The presence of your Christ

Abba:

Unwrap the layers of my heart in these Advent days so I can more clearly see the presence of your Christ in both friend and stranger.

Amen.

December 2
Your appearing in others

Loving God:

I make this my prayer today. I wish to know your closeness. I will watch for your appearing in others and say with Mary, "Let it be with me according to your word."

Amen.

December 3
I await your return to the world

Lord Jesus Christ:

I give my heart to the loving attention of your living presence within. Help me build my life upon the security of your Word in this uncertain world. I confess I need Christmas to remind me that you are with me. Enduring and eternal, your Spirit upholds all things and dwells within.

Be born again through me. In this surrendered heart, I await your return to the world.

Amen.

December 4
A gift of mercy

Living Christ:

I wish to be a gift of mercy and compassion today. You, O Lord Christ, are here, calling me into love and holiness.

Amen.

December 5
May this Advent season crescendo

Living God of the Liturgy:

May this Advent season crescendo with luminosity, bearing the light of Christ made beautiful by love through humbled hearts.

No longer just through poetry or song, I awake to your birth in me today. Infused with Christmas beauty, I feel your loving presence. Your prophets are calling. You are preparing a space for grace in me. I willingly surrender.

Amen.

December 6
The shelter of the living Christ

God of the Humble:

With Mary, the mother of Jesus, I dedicate my inner being to the shelter of the living Christ.

Encircle me with your Spirit of life and bring to bear through me this day a further incarnation of light, life, and love.

Amen.

December 7
I ride the moment into the future

Beloved of My Lifetime:

My heart is alive with a desire reflected in the nighttime heavens. Alive, awake, shining, I ride the moment into the future with a faith grounded in that first kiss from your love, when as a child I looked up and saw a shooting star and felt a falling snowflake come to rest on my cheek.

Amen.

December 8
We the simple and unadorned

Lord Jesus, Living Christ:

Let it be in us according to your Word.

We the simple and unadorned.

We the masses.

We the worker bees.

We the day laborers for life.

We the weary mothers and fathers.

We with calloused hands and soft hearts.

We shall be your glorious temple, and we will practice today with prayer.

Amen.

December 9
Alert for the celebration

Coming King of Love:

I wish to feel your living presence in and through me in these Advent days, to be alert for the celebration of your birth, then, now, and yet to be.

I choose a conscious Christmas, attentive to your Word in me and not to the chatter of our culture.

Amen.

December 10
The light, life, and love of my inner world

Light of the World:

May shames lurking in the underside of my soul be revealed in the presence of your light.

May sorrows heavy-laden upon my heart be relieved by the presence of your life.

May shadows cast by gnarled memories be smoothed out in the presence of your love.

Through and in Christ, who is the light, life, and love of my inner world.

Amen.

December 11
I will not fear

Faithful God:

Whatever happens in the world, your light of wisdom and love endures. In this partnership with humankind, you provide strength, safety, and sustenance. Therefore, I will not fear. I celebrate and light my candles of faith.

Amen.

December 12
Inspired by your initiative

Divine Love:

Pour into the vessel of my heart the presence of love for you and others. Inspired by your initiative, I choose to become a living gift of love today. Freed from all compulsion to pay for or demand proof of another's worthiness, I simply offer the gift of love, in word, deed, and countenance.

Amen.

December 13
I await your light of the world

Lord Jesus, Living Christ:

Each day I draw further into the deepening darkness. I await your light of the world. The darkness has its limits. The light will rise again.

I give to you, Lord Jesus Christ, my self-contained fears and desires; while my interior remains hidden to others, it remains open to the light of your love.

Amen.

December 14
Taste the joy no red wine can give

God of Miraculous Events:

In the darkness of these days, I enter the center of the flame of your Christ's love. In this light, I open to your love and taste the joy no red wine can give.

More alive than ever, I pray not to spend my days curled up on the inside with resentment. Help me live with an open heart bearing love in ordinary ways.

Amen.

December 15
Jesus's birth is a demonstration

God of Wondrous Ways:

In the confusion of commerce and over years of mythmaking, it is easy for my mind to wander from the intention of Christmas. Open my heart and mind to the truth hiding in plain sight: Jesus's birth is a demonstration of how much humanity means to you.

In him, your love embraced humanity.

In him, nothing can now separate us from your love.

I surrender to your continuing incarnation through me.

Amen.

December 16

Your love is vast, infinite, and available

Lord God of All Creation:

The longest night nears, but so too does your light in Christ.

For all my moments of stress spent shopping or in crowds, I receive your peace.

For all those who wonder how to make ends meet, I request your provision.

For all those who feel lonely, I request your loving presence.

All is well, beyond every perception to the contrary. Help me see how your love is vast, infinite, and available in the tender darkness of surrender, prayer, and praise.

Amen.

December 17

An interior Christmas

Lord Jesus, Living Christ:

Your mystery is not solved by asking questions. It is felt and opened.

I request the personal experience of your continuing presence. Lead me from confusion to clarity through the silence.

You are as near as the love I feel in my chest. You are as close as the laughter in my belly. You are with me as the light for thought and breath for life.

Today I choose an interior Christmas, connected in my body to Bethlehem and with heaven in my heart.

Amen.

December 18
The glorious impossible

God of Possibilities:

A week from today I will pause and watch children, friends, and family open presents. It will be Christmas Day. All my preparations will be complete.

I give you every concern that overwhelms and every relationship that is rusty. I invite your possibilities to continue in my life and loved ones. In your grace, do the glorious impossible.

Amen.

December 19
Shadows cast by traumas past

Light of the World:

May your Word reveal to me the path to wisdom and love in all my relationships and choices.

Where there is darkness in my personality and shadows cast by traumas past or anxieties present, ever so gently illumine these opportunities in the light of your silent grace.

Amen.

December 20
The mystery of your first Christmas

Beloved of Bethlehem:

A few days from today, Lord, I will grow silent in awe of the mystery of your first Christmas. Help me prepare to receive your living Word again.

Amen.

December 21

I enter into the deepest days of darkness

Light of the World, Glory of the Heavens:

I enter the deepest days of darkness in this season of lights and love.

I anticipate the coming of your Christ declared by prophets and recalled through story—and occurring now in my receptive heart of faith.

Help me connect more deeply with your love for humankind in Christ.

Give me courage to be the love that Jesus bore witness to and invites all of us to become.

Amen.

December 22

I offer my total being to your total grace

All Praise to You, O God of Love:

I offer my total being to your total grace.

With Mary, I wish to sing a song of love's freedom, of light's wisdom, of life's unfolding.

By your overshadowing Spirit of creation let my will, imagination, and memory become virgin again.

Let water, sky, and earth become virgin again.

Let a second innocence return, now christened with the consciousness of two thousand years of life experience in the age of Eucharist and Spirit.

I see that our ways of division, war, greed, and fear were never nor will ever be useful to the destiny of our becoming.

Let this Advent prepare me and the world in the most practical ways to go deeper into the self being born by your Word to a united destiny in love.

Amen.

December 23

Deeper into your story of love

Abba:

I lift my dreams to you. Help me listen for your leading in the stillness of my sleep. Prepare my life to receive your Word again. Help me see deeper into your story of love and participate with faith.

Amen.

December 24

This ecstasy of love moves through eternity into time

God of My Lifetime:

The sound of silence opens into song, with stars leading to the light of the world made visible in the field of flesh and form.

This ecstasy of love moves through eternity into time, to be for us the hope of love lived to give all for all.

Opening us, the gift rises through the centuries, undoing the self that strikes out in fear, judgment, and wanting.

Freed to love, we now can sing the song of silence:

Hosanna to God in the highest. Your love triumphs through humility. Our soul knows its worth and falls on its knees. Silent night, holy night, your new song sings me!

Amen!

December 25
Christmas is for love

God of Bethlehem:

Christmas is for love.

Christmas is love.

Christmas is.

Christmas.

Christ.

Love.

I welcome your divine love and blessings to, for, and in all ways of being human.

Amen!

December 26

Encircled by eternity

Sphere of Being, Dancing Love:

Encircled by eternity, lift me up into your love. Flowing through existence is your living and active Word, sustaining and upholding all things, including me. I am part of your fabric of divine intention, a participant of your holy web of emerging life. I consent to the victory of love in Christ, then, now, and always.

Amen.

December 27
I turn my heart to the warmth of your love

Source of Song and Light of Love:

I lift my silence in praise to you.

You hold the mysteries of the heavens and manifest the gift of light through all suns and stars above and sons and daughters below. May your kingdom come on earth as it is in the heavens.

On this winter day, I turn my heart to the warmth of your love to melt away the barriers to your way and will. In my simple and silent surrender, help me become what I already am: your light-bearing heir.

Amen.

December 28
Your faithfulness is occurring

Unending Strength of Love:

When I am faced with mounting debts, sickness, or personal difficulties it is easy to forget that you, my God, are working. Help me to see that your faithfulness is occurring, despite my inability or unwillingness to perceive under the surface, the mystery of your glory rising through my temporary suffering or lack.

Amen.

December 29

Connecting through wholeness the many into one body

Loving God with Us:

Open my heart and mind to feel your presence and my existence in you. Help me release fears, wants, and judgments that separate others into parts and perceptions limiting my experience of oneness with you and others.

Draw me into the hidden life of Christ who is all in all, connecting through wholeness the many into one body of love, bringing to all the personal quality of presence in and acceptance of that which is occurring right now.

Amen.

December 30

The speed of seasons coming to their full

Voice of Silence:

I wait for your hand to move at the speed of seasons coming to their full in the perfect synchronicity of divine providence, tuned to the time of unfolding grace meeting me face to face in Scripture and silence.

Amen.

December 31

An imprint of wholeness in community

Lord God Almighty:

At the conclusion of this year, it's as if you are saying to me, "Plumb the silence and find me. Explore my grace and discover yourself again. Rest in me and watch me do my miracles in the life from me that is now your own."

And my heart cries out: O my Beloved! Unveil the secret of your hidden love at the center of my being. Turn this new year into a time and space for oneness—with you, with others, and with the real "I" in me who wishes to be born through the multiplicity of my persona.

Beyond just me, birth the real "us" that can be for the world an imprint of wholeness in community held by the bond of your love, vivified by the warmth of your good, true, and Holy Spirit.

Amen.

Prayers for HOLY DAYS *and* SEASONS

Through the Seasons in Love and Silence

Day encircles light,
Night the scarce space.

Linger with me at center;
feel my life become yours,
and then mine again.

I whisper your name
underneath the rock's silence;
everlasting is their resting.

Come to me and listen.
My heart presses upon your waiting.

This is home,
Together.

ADVENT

And the Spirit Says:

Take my hand and feel the grip of nothing that holds everything with light and moves with grace and slight rhythms.

Take my hand and release your grip on everything else, grasping at nothing but surrender.

And in your empty palms pressed together at the heart, feel the arrival of love's warmth as fear and other such soul-fevers slip through clasped hands of desire.

Take the hands of everyone else and place them to your face, as a blind beggar looking for someone long lost; remember who you are and what all life is for.

I am the hand of God worn smooth with loving touches caressed in prayer—empty always, yet filled with giving. I am left and right; presence and absence; illumination and transformation.

I am two hands, building a temple for your wishes.
I use every tear for mortar, every laugh for stone.

These hands are ceaseless, though never weary. They move out over all things as wind, wisdom, light, song.

And hold fast to you now, always, in right or wrong.

Amen.

CHRISTMAS

Word made flesh;
Life refreshed.
Love, to us now given.
God drew near;
Joy, not fear.
Love, to us now given.
Wonder how?
Heart must bow.
Love, to us now given.
Enter King;
Miracle gifts bring.
Love, to us now given.

Wrapped in words;
Opened when heard.
Love, to us now given.
Word for me;
Stable to Tree.
Love, to us now given.

I am part of your living Word from the beginning. Perhaps this might change my plans for today—or even for tomorrow. I ponder and listen again to the ancient gift hidden within me—and wish to be opened by your love:

My body, Bethlehem.

My mind, a manger.

My heart, a hymn of praise in tempo with your Spirit.

Amen.

NEW YEAR'S EVE

Lord Jesus Christ:

With you, I journey.

In your humanity, I am.

In your divinity, I shall be.

Released from the maze of memories written in the past, I am lifted into a renewed freedom to love.

Drawn to you by the magnetism of grace, I conclude this year with gratitude, and begin the New Year trusting your faithfulness to bring about my deepest aims.

Amen.

ASH WEDNESDAY

God of Transformation:

You set our hearts on fire with the personal touch of your Spirit enfolding truth into our minds as an impression of wisdom.

You enliven us with your love that we know beyond knowing. Your unstoppable impulse to share your life with us is available to us at this moment.

Amen.

PALM SUNDAY

And now, O God of perfect timing, enter each of our hearts and find the city-center in us ready to receive and surrender to your love in its embodied form and in its eternal formlessness.

We have been preparing for the entrance of your Word through this Lenten journey and now we feel your timeless approach nearing. What are you calling us to do? What more can we surrender of our self? How can we live with this exquisite wound of love that suffering teaches?

This city-center is the ongoing temple of our heart, mind, and soul, today arranged and set apart to celebrate your arrival.

Your way shows us that soon your arrival will require surrender, and in this surrender, there will be great suffering.

Yet so too your truth shows us that in this suffering there will be something gained on behalf of others, and through this gain of love a power untold will pierce through the field of appearances and birth a new life through all that is dead and dying in us.

And so it is that your life is felt more fully in our welcoming all things, but especially the body and blood of the Eucharist as the ongoing teacher and embrace of your joyful presence.

Amen.

MAUNDY THURSDAY

Lord God of All Creation:

Every night reminds us of the darkness that we can't escape, yet tonight the darkness is particularly deep.

Infused with betrayal, laced with denial, sealed with the cup, marked with Gethsemane blood, you, Lord Jesus Christ, embraced surrender while rejecting the way of the sword.

You entered the valley of the shadow of death, meeting betrayal, denial, rejection, conviction, and abandonment in order to join human nature in the depths of its dysfunction and rejection of love.

If evil is the denial of the reality of God, then sin is a way of life based on the unreality of God, who is love. Tonight, we prepare to see the depths of unreality: unbelief, hatred, and violence.

Lord Jesus, the drama is enacted in your life to show us what is in our life, and in its exposing to the light of your surrendering yet pursuing love, we hear the clank of keys coming down the dark prison hallway of the night that lets the prisoners know they can be free. It sounds like this: "Father, forgive them, for they know not what they do."

Amen.

GOOD FRIDAY

My God, My God of All My Why's:

It is now finished. This is the hour. The moment when selfhood became lost into your hands, and your hands became remembered in a human body. One with you in Jesus, humanity can never be separated again.

I need not wonder how it is done, I only request the grace to surrender to let it be done unto me: dead to self, alive to you.

Amen.

HOLY SATURDAY

Lord Jesus, Living Christ:

On your inward journey into the depths of being and beyond, reveal in each of us the places where there are still captives that need to hear your story and be set free. Descend all the way down into the thinking and doing that is resistant to your love. We need your help to be raised back to life not just tomorrow but right now, finally set free from our self-bound ways of fear and falseness. From that moment of integration with your love, we will truly live. You are indeed our hope of true glory, then, now, and always.

Amen.

EASTER SUNDAY

O God of the Light, Bearer of the Heavens:

In our world of death, suffering, and sorrow, you have sounded a new octave of life, reverberating through the cosmos in each dimension and direction. Give me the full capacity to consent to this signal sound permeating with the harmonics of love, seen and unseen. I wish to not only hear it but also be the very vessel in which the sound is turned into form.

Stabilize me with the wisdom of Scripture and the strength of community so that I am not undone by the glory of the event.

In Christ, nothing can separate me from the love of God.

Amen.

PENTECOST

Holy Spirit of God:

I rest in your continued anointing.

By your Spirit, guide my intellect to perfectly see and know.

Direct my will to harmoniously choose and act.

Open my heart to relentlessly love and serve.

Since through Christ by the Spirit you are in me and I am in you, connect me also with others so that your kingdom might come again through us, your living body of light continuing on this earthly sojourn.

Amen.

THANKSGIVING

O God Who Sustains All in Every Way:

Over the circled space of this earthly orb since I've last gathered to give thanks, I look to the depths and see reasons both clearly and dimly to doubt the goodness of life—sickness, pain, suffering, disaster, depression, layoffs, and diagnosis. All have been in our midst.

Holding hands with my beloveds, I feel the assurance that we are more alive together than apart. I sense the common human bond of being, this gift that rises and falls yet never ceases to teach and woo us into our God-intended destiny.

Opening to you in this silence of prayer, I let go of the resentments. I release the tears that mark the forgotten stories. I reconcile with the losses, the damage, the baggage, and the prodigals. I am welcomed home in this love made manifest together. I am one part of the woven tapestry story of your total grace.

In the bond of the breath of God, in this name sealed upon my heart in gratitude, I say "Yes!" by saying "Thank you!"

Amen.

AT A TIME OF DEATH

Nearing the door of death, greet me with Your loving light. I hope to hear your ocean song calling me home, and all that has not been done is surrendered. Help me recognize that I am free to sink away into the depths of your love, no longer just as me, but also as another wave returning home to you.

Amen.

AT A TIME OF DECISION

In the silence may your Word wake me with the light of love guiding my way home. Help me remember who I am and recognize my fears as shadows dispelled by the dawn of your wisdom drawing near to my heart.

Amen.

Books

Richard J. Foster and Emilie Griffin, eds. *Spiritual Classics: Selected Readings on the Twelve Spiritual Disciplines*. New York: HarperCollins, 2000.

Nan C. Merrill, *Psalms for Praying: An Invitation to Wholeness*. New York: Continuum, 2008.

Internet

www.ContemplativeChristians.com
www.ContemplativeOutreach.org

January 30

An event inspired this prayer: I spoke with a young husband who told me that as he was driving to the hospital at four in the morning to see his wife, who was in cardiac arrest, he heard her voice as the car radio came on. Her voice said, "Beloved, I must go now." It was 4:42 a.m. Later, when he was speaking with the doctors, they confirmed that it was at that precise time that his wife died.

May 1

Nan C. Merrill, *Psalms for Praying: An Invitation to Wholeness* (New York: Continuum, 2008). Adapted from Psalm 31.

June 17

The first four "Let me" lines of this prayer are inspired by the contemplative Bernadette Roberts, who shared this during a private retreat in Fullerton, California, November 7, 2010. She said that this is the prayer she says with her grandchildren as she tucks them into bed.

July 3

Adapted from the Carmina Gadelica prayer "Encompassing," in Esther De Waal, *The Celtic Way of Prayer* (New York: Doubleday, 1999).

August 1

Merrill, *Psalms for Praying*. Adapted prayer from Psalm 88.

Rev. Dr. Peter Traben Haas is an ordained Teaching Pastor in the Presbyterian Church (USA) and serves as the senior pastor at a contemplative Christian church and community located in Austin, Texas. Peter earned a B.A. from Moody Bible, an M.Div. from Princeton Seminary and a Doctorate of Ministry from Austin Presbyterian Theological Seminary. Peter serves as an Adjunct Faculty member at The Seminary of the Southwest and is a certified Centering Prayer instructor and retreat leader. The author of multiple books and articles on the contemplative Christian dimension, Peter is an oblate of the New Camaldoli Hermitage in Big Sur, California.

ABOUT PARACLETE PRESS

Paraclete Press is the publishing arm of the Cape Cod Benedictine community, the Community of Jesus. Presenting a full expression of Christian belief and practice, we reflect the ecumenical charism of the Community and its dedication to sacred music, the fine arts, and the written word.

SCAN TO READ MORE

www.paracletepress.com